Alfred Elwes

Through Spain by Rail in 1872

Alfred Elwes

Through Spain by Rail in 1872

ISBN/EAN: 9783337246082

Printed in Europe, USA, Canada, Australia, Japan

Cover: Foto ©Andreas Hilbeck / pixelio.de

More available books at **www.hansebooks.com**

THROUGH SPAIN BY RAIL

IN

1872.

BY

ALFRED ELWES.

LONDON:
EFFINGHAM WILSON, ROYAL EXCHANGE.
1873.

TO

ROBERT W. WILKINSON, Esq.,

THIS WORK IS INSCRIBED

AS

A SLIGHT PROOF

OF

FRIENDSHIP AND ESTEEM.

PREFACE.

Spain has had the advantage of being depicted by many and able pens. The charming and finished sketches of Washington Irving, the caustic, humorous, and exhaustive pages of Ford, will be fresh in the minds of thousands of English readers; and those who wish to study the treasures of architecture of the Iberian Peninsula may do so, with greater profit than heretofore, through the valuable productions of Street and others.

The object of the present work is of a different and humbler character, and is sufficiently explained by its title-page. The letters which compose it were written on the spot, when the impressions they seek to convey were fresh upon the mind; and, if they possess no other merit, I may at least claim for them that of being a faithful transcript of the places they describe.

A. E.

BRIGHTON;
   March, 1873.

CONTENTS.

LETTER I.
BRIGHTON TO PARIS *via* DIEPPE.—Newhaven—Dieppe
—Paris 1

LETTER II.
PARIS TO BORDEAUX.—Paris—The Mi-carême—The Valley of the Loire—Blois—Poitiers—Bordeaux . 5

LETTER III.
AT BORDEAUX. — Bordeaux — A Fair—The Théâtre Français 9

LETTER IV.
BORDEAUX TO BIARRITZ.—The Landes—Pine Forests—Bayonne—Biarritz—Secluded Situation . . 12

LETTER V.
AT BIARRITZ. — General Aspect of Biarritz—Villa Eugénie—Bareness of Trees . . . 17

LETTER VI.
BIARRITZ TO BURGOS.—Entrance into Spain—First Appearance of the Country—Spade Husbandry—Troublesome Examination of Luggage—Miranda—Arrival at Burgos—A Spanish Fonda—Spanish Beggars—The Cathedral—Spanish Houses—Public Promenade 22

LETTER VII.

BURGOS TO VALLADOLID.—Aspect of the Country—Country Towns—Valladolid—Hotel Service—The Museum—Cathedral—Silversmiths' Shops—The Market Place 38

LETTER VIII.

VALLADOLID TO MADRID.—Sterile Scenery—A Stony Tract—Large Olive Trees—View of the Escorial—Arrival at Madrid 46

LETTER IX.

MADRID.—Spanish Cookery—Good Bread—First Appearance of Madrid—Its Streets—Soldiers—Military Music 53

LETTER X.

MADRID.—A Missing Letter—Spanish Post-Office and its Officials—Cigarette-Smoking—Madrid Houses—Puerta del Sol—Spanish Women—Casas de Huespedes 57

LETTER XI.

MADRID.—The Museum of Pictures—The Spanish School—Velasquez—Murillo—Ribera—Juanes—Coello—Zurbaran—Specimens of the Italian School 65

LETTER XII.

MADRID.—A Dreary Evening—The Opera House of Madrid—King Amadeo—The Prado—Paseo de los Recolletos—The Wet-nurses of Madrid . . 72

LETTER XIII.

MADRID.—The Manzanares—Laundresses of Madrid—Bridges—Mules and Donkeys—Dogs—Beggars—Their Guitars—The Lottery . . . 81

LETTER XIV.

MADRID.—Variations of Atmosphere—Umbrellas—A Wander Round the City—Dos de Mayo—Plaza Mayor 88

CONTENTS. ix

LETTER XV.

PAGE

MADRID.—A Trip to the Escorial—The Approach from Madrid — Enormous Extent — Strange Design— The Chapel—The Pantheon . . . 93

LETTER XVI.

MADRID TO SARAGOSSA.—The Road to Saragossa— Ancient Cities—Alcalá de Henares—Guadalajara —The Henares Canal — Sigüenza covered with Snow—The Moors—Calatayud—Arrival at Saragossa—An Old Acquaintance . . . 101

LETTER XVII.

SARAGOSSA.—Aspect of the Streets—Ancient Houses —El Coso — The Casino—The Aljaferia — Two Cathedrals—The Ebro—Spanish Markets . . 107

LETTER XVIII.

PAMPLONA.—Difficulties of Spanish Travel—The *Real* Interest of Spain—Pamplona—Fine Situation and Picturesqueness—Tudela— Tafalla—Olite—Beautiful Moorish Ruin 114

LETTER XIX.

SARAGOSSA —Good Friday strictly observed—Leaning Tower—Costume of Country People—Beggars —Frightful Cripples—Waiting for the Procession 122

LETTER XX.

SARAGOSSA.—The Easter Procession—Lay Figures— A Country Drive—Impossibility of Residing away from the City—A Desolate Estate—A Picturesque Guard. 127

LETTER XXI.

SARAGOSSA.—A Bull Fight 135

LETTER XXII.

SARAGOSSA TO BARCELONA.—Companionship by the Way — Lerida — Manresa — Montserrat — Grand Appearance—A Splendid Prospect—Arrival at

Barcelona—Beautiful Situation—Busy Aspect of its Streets and Shops—Cathedral—View of the City from Montjuis 145

LETTER XXIII.

BARCELONA TO TARRAGONA.—Environs of Barcelona—Fine Mountain Scenery—Lofty Situation of Tarragona—Picturesque Houses—Cathedral—Cloisters—Roman Aqueduct—Party Spirit . . . 152

LETTER XXIV.

REUS.—Uneasy Pavement—General Dulness—Appearance of the Country 162

LETTER XXV.

TARRAGONA TO VALENCIA.—Richness of Vegetation—Tedious Travelling—Orange Plantations—Their Wealth—Cathedral—Absence of Monks and Friars 166

LETTER XXVI.

VALENCIA.—Effects of Irrigation—Train Stopped by Brigands—The Alameda—Splendid "Plaza de Toros" 173

LETTER XXVII.

VALENCIA TO MADRID.—Festival of San Vicente, the Patron of Valencia—View from Summit of San Miguel—Orange Plantations—Wonderful Fertility—Alcina—Feast of Roses—La Encina—Aranjuez—Fine View of Madrid 177

LETTER XXVIII.

MADRID.—General Remarks on Travelling through Spain—Country singularly Uninteresting—Causes of Sterility 183

LETTER XXIX.

MADRID.—A Charming Picture—A Villa in the Prado—Dislike of the Spaniards to the Country—An English Dinner—Rudeness of the Madrileños towards the King—Inner Life of the Spaniards . 189

CONTENTS.

LETTER XXX.

MADRID TO CORDOVA.—Don Quixote's Country—Wildness of the Road—Rich Colours of the Flowers—Linares—Menjibar—Cordova—Its Narrow Streets and Moorish Buildings—Charming *Patios*—Court of Oranges—The Mesquita—Andalusian Women . 197

LETTER XXXI.

SEVILLE.—Road from Cordova to Seville—Oranges and Aloes—Mosquitoes—Andalusian and Gypsy Dances — Cathedral — The Giralda — Pompeian Arrangements 207

LETTER XXXII.

SEVILLE. — The Alcazar— Beautiful Azulejos— The Gardens—Exhibition of Modern Paintings—The City Walls—House of Pilatus—The Museo—The Women of Seville—Alameda . . . 220

LETTER XXXIII.

XERES (SHERRY). — Fellow-Travellers — Arrival at Xerez—Peculiarity of Xerez Houses—Love-making —Wine Stores 230

LETTER XXXIV.

CADIZ.—Vineyards—Salt-pans—First Appearance of Cadiz—Street Sights—Mules—Glazed Balconies—Custom-House Arrangements — Charming Alameda 237

LETTER XXXV.

GIBRALTAR.—Bay of Cadiz—The Voyage—Trafalgar —Tarifa — Algesiras— Confusion at Landing—Transformation Scene 249

LETTER XXXVI.

GIBRALTAR.—Visit to the Rock—Fine Views—The Signal Battery—The Apes—Wealth of Vegetation —Cockney Houses , ... 256

LETTER XXXVII.

MALAGA.— Rough Passage—The Carabineers— Marbilla—Difficulties of Landing—Aspects of the

xii   CONTENTS.

                                                                                                 PAGE

Town— Narrowness of the Streets — Want of Drainage— Democratic Behaviour — Cathedral— Fine View 263

LETTER XXXVIII.

MALAGA TO GRANADA.—Slowness of Travelling—The Diligence Journey— Picturesque Group—Beauty of Country outside Malaga—Alora—Arrival at Loja—A Mishap—First Impression of the Alhambra 273

LETTER XXXIX.

THE ALHAMBRA.—Visit to the Palace of the Alhambra —Impressions—Fine Views—The Tocador de la Reina—The Baths—P. V. 285

LETTER XL.

THE ALHAMBRA.—Charming situation of the Alhambra—A Visit by Moonlight—Peris at the Gate of Paradise—Beautiful Effects of Light— Fascination of the Alhambra—The Gypsies . . 296

LETTER XLI.

GRANADA.—Cathedral—Capilla de los Reyes—Tombs of Ferdinand and Isabella—The Cartuja—The Zacatin— Gil Blas—The Generalife — Beautiful Situation—La Silla del Moro . . . 306

LETTER XLII.

FROM GRANADA TO TOLEDO.—Political Rumours— Another Diligence Journey—Solitude of Spanish Landscape—Jaen—Menjibar—Alcazar—Castillejo —First Appearance of Toledo—Ancient Houses— Decay and picturesqueness 317

LETTER XLIII.

MADRID.—Political Troubles—Uneasy Feeling in the Capital –Petty Conduct of the Grandees—The Male Population—In the Country and at Madrid 329

LETTER XLIV.

MADRID TO PARIS.—Quiet Journey Northward—An Old Acquaintance—His views of the State of Spain —Advancing Spring—Closing Remarks . . 337.

THROUGH SPAIN BY RAIL

IN THE SPRING OF 1872.

LETTER I.

BRIGHTON TO PARIS *viá* DIEPPE.

NEWHAVEN—DIEPPE—ROUEN—PARIS.

> Hôtel du Louvre, Paris;
> *March* 7, 1872.

I ARRIVED at Newhaven in time to wait two hours before the starting of the boat, which did not leave till half-past eleven p.m. A tradesman's ball was being held at the Hotel, which did not tend to the comfort of travellers, who were turned out of coffee- and smoking-rooms into a musty back-parlour; nor could they be expected to be consoled by enlivening music for their want of comfort, as they could hear it only by snatches, and then only the louder and more discordant notes.

As the wind had been blowing rather freshly from the south-east, I expected, with, I believe, the majority of my fellow-passengers, that there would be a heavy sea outside the harbour. This, however, was not the case, for the steamer glided almost imperceptibly from the shelter of the piers into the open channel, nor was there any movement to speak of during the crossing.

The French coast was reached too early to enter the port of Dieppe and we were compelled to lay to for upwards of an hour. At length the appearance of the white funnels of the sister steamer issuing from the harbour on her voyage to Newhaven showed us that the tide was at a sufficient height, and we steamed in accordingly.

The old town of Dieppe presented much the same appearance as usual as we drove round to the railway station where we had time for breakfast and a good deal to spare after it, the train not starting till nearly eight.

All the clear sky we had been enjoying at Brighton during the last few days had quite abandoned us long ere this, and we ran through the pretty valley of the Seine with that accompaniment of wet mist for which Normandy is not unjustly celebrated. The rain, however, could not take from the picturesqueness of many of the old towns and villages we passed by. Rouen looked as beautiful as ever, both on approaching and leaving it. You remember how fine a glimpse you get of the ancient city when, on emerging from the last tunnel, you cross the Seine and behold the bridge and clustering towers of the capital through a framework of terraced gardens on the right, and the green island and velvety meadows on the left. The picture wanted sunshine, but not even a gloomy sky could take from its beauty, which was enjoyed to the full by some of my fellow-passengers who saw it for the first time.

The Louvre is fuller than when you and I were here last October, and they are even engaged upon a little painting and cleaning.

But it will be long, I fancy, before they see return those palmy days of the Second Empire, when a place at the *table d'hôte* was unattainable unless bespoken in the morning.

LETTER II.

PARIS TO BORDEAUX.

PARIS—THE MI-CARÊME—THE VALLEY OF THE LOIRE—
BLOIS—POITIERS—BORDEAUX.

Hôtel de la Paix, Bordeaux;
March 9, 1872.

I HOPE you got my letter from Paris, as it will have relieved your mind about my comfort during the crossing and first part of my journey. After I had despatched it, although the rain kept falling, I *flanéed* about the streets and discovered from the masks in various states of "bedraggledness" that it was the *mi-carême,* or mid-lent. The groups I saw were chiefly composed of students and *ouvriers,* who amused themselves with the loudest "charivaris" of discordant instruments. At night there was a masked-ball at the opera, and entertainments of a similar character were given in other less reputable places. The *fun* was kept up till daybreak, and, as I heard from an eye-witness next morning, extraordinary scenes of debauchery were going on all night.

I gladly left Paris yesterday morning at 10.45 a.m. for this city, and after a not unpleasant journey I arrived at my hotel here a little before 11 at night. The sky had such delicious patches of blue at times, and the air felt so light and agreeable, that I thought I was about at once to revel in sunshine, but before the train had got a hundred miles upon its course, heavy, black clouds discharged torrents of rain, and it has continued raining from that hour to the present, although it is not now falling heavily.

The valley of the Loire, through which the train conveys you at a capital pace, offers some very fine views. It is particularly rich in châteaux, which appear pile above pile with round towers and extinguisher tops—half château, half fortress. That of Amboise is especially striking. The vines are very abundant before reaching Blois, and continue from that district throughout the journey.

The city of Tours, for some time the seat of the government when driven out of Paris in 1870, looks very pretty as you get a glimpse of it up the Loire from the train, and Poitiers, famous in English history, is remarkably so, being perched on rocky heights, which must make its streets wonderfully up and down. There is a rapid stream, the Clain, which should yield good trout, running at the base of the rocks, and then rushing through green meadows and past rich, red banks, reminding me of parts of Devonshire.

After dining at Angoulême at seven, the rest of the journey was performed in darkness, Bordeaux being reached at a quarter-past ten—as true to time as the French express trains generally are.

Bordeaux is decidedly a fine, well-built city, looking very substantial with its square stone houses and many fine broad streets.

The Grand Theatre, which, as you may remember, was used by the French Government at the end of 1870 for holding its sittings when the advancing Prussians made Tours too hot to be pleasant, is as fine a building of the kind as you will see, more imposing in outward appearance than the Scala at Milan, or the San Carlo at Naples. A spacious colonnade running round it, supported by lofty pillars of stone, contributes very much to the grandeur of the edifice.

This letter will, I reckon, be delivered to you about the time I am entering Spain. Up to this point the travelling has been as expeditious as one could wish, and I find myself 364 miles south of Paris without being sensible of any fatigue. Once, however, over the border, and I expect all will be changed. I wish I could be sure of always getting such comfortable clean beds as I had at the Louvre, and find here. Still I will not anticipate discomforts, but determine rather, when they come—and come they will, if I am to believe all the accounts I hear—to meet them with due patience and resignation.

LETTER III.

AT BORDEAUX.

BORDEAUX—A FAIR—THE THÉÂTRE FRANÇAIS.

Bordeaux;
March 9, 1872.

IN spite of the rain I have been wandering about the streets of this fine old city, which has a somewhat modern look, in spite of its antiquity. I managed to get to the Place des Quinconces, a grand and regular square, opening at one end, where there are two huge pillars with naval trophies in the Roman style, on to the Quay, which is said to run for three miles along the banks of the Garonne. Here I found a huge fair was being held, a true "Greenwich" and "Old Charlton" concern, with its circus, its Richardson's Theatre (a *French* Richardson, of course), its Wombwell's Menagerie, swings, roundabouts, fat women (plenty of the latter), *et hoc genus omne*

The Place, however, is so vast that there was no crowding, and the only noisy people were those on the stages of the various booths, the spectators looking on in a very tranquil, not to say apathetic manner. The rain, perhaps, had damped their spirits.

In the evening I visited the Théâtre Français, where I sat one piece, "Papillonne," through, and the first act of another, "Un Troupier qui suit les Bonnes." Both these pieces derive the little interest they possess from their gross immorality. If we are to accept such comedies as a reflex of French manners, we must look upon French society as rotten to the core. But I am sure it would be doing gross injustice to take such view. I must believe that there is virtue and there is continence in France as elsewhere—otherwise, the institution of marriage would, of a certainty, cease to exist; for who would care to give his name to a woman and his time and labour to the support of a family when his wife welcomes to her arms the first bold *intriguant*, and he cannot be certain the children are his own? The writers who so depict their countrymen and women I consider to be calumniators. Surely life offers sufficient variety and interest to charm an audience with the representation of its phases without presenting to the public eye scenes which are a disgrace to civilized society.

LETTER IV.

BORDEAUX TO BIARRITZ.

THE LANDES—PINE FORESTS—BAYONNE—BIARRITZ—
SECLUDED SITUATION.

Biarritz;
March 10, 1872.

I WAS up at six this morning to pursue my journey southwards, the weather still lowering, and followed, as the day came on, by the rain which has hitherto accompanied me. I observed the ill effects of all this wet on driving to the station. The river had swollen over the quays and set various articles floating, and if the south-easterly gales, which have been so prevalent recently, do not abate, the damage may become considerable.

The road was flat and uninteresting, that is, as regards scenery, and owing to vegetation being but little advanced, the skeletons of the trees looked cold and dreary. There were forests of pine and deserts of sand covered with stunted briars and the withered leaves of the bracken fern. The pines were almost all tapped for resin—long strips of bark had been sliced off to a height of ten or twelve feet from the ground, and one, two, or three little earthen pots were fixed to the bare places to receive the fatty matter as it exuded from the wound.

In passing through these extensive *Landes* I looked out for the shepherds on stilts, but saw only one, a mere lad by a cottage door. I can well understand, however, the necessity of such "continuations" to perambulate these desert plains of sand and scrub which looked particularly miserable and sterile under the gloomy sky and falling rain.

The guard-houses of the railway, which are painted red and are châlet shaped, were almost the only habitations visible for fifty miles together. Where the soil allowed of it little gardens had been laid out in their vicinity, and although they were in themselves nothing to look at, the blossom of the peach, almond, and pear, made them appear like oases in the desert.

On approaching Bayonne I saw some fine olive trees, the lower portion of their trunks, say, for some six feet, being stripped of its bark. At Bayonne I caught my first glimpse of the Atlantic, looking very yellow and threatening, a strong breeze blowing at the time; and twenty minutes afterwards I was deposited at the station of this little town, almost the only passenger. Fortunately, I found a conveyance to bring me on, though the rogue of a coachman charged me five francs for the accommodation,—but it was impossible to do without him as I was encumbered with luggage, and the station is nearly two miles distant from the town.

The road is a good one, bordered by banks sprinkled with wild violets—very pretty although scentless—the hedges are all exhibiting their fresh green—and many of the early trees are in leaf. The weather, however, is as bad as ever; a strong cold breeze blowing over the ocean, charged with rain, and the sky as gloomy as ever it looks in England, although I am as far south as Florence.

You descend into Biarritz by rather a steep road, and when you get there you find yourself in an irregularly built but clean little place on the border of the Bay of Biscay, far removed from the noise and turmoil of the great world.

It reminds me somewhat of Ilfracombe, with the exception that the rocks are dark sand colour instead of being nearly black, and that there are not so many of them. The bathing must be very delicious, for there are little bays with soft shelving sand, and an *établissement* at the head of each for the convenience of the bathers. In the summer I should think it must be a delightful retreat, for there are plenty of quaint houses with bits of terraces and gardens in every direction; but with a few notable exceptions, the dwellings give you an idea of having been run up in a hurry, for though they are substantial enough they look rough and unpolished.

There was a magnificent sea on, and I stood in a sheltered nook out of the rain to watch the big billows play in and out the caverns they have worn for themselves in the sandstone rocks with a noise like thunder. The most has been made out of every jutting cliff, for there are pathways leading round and over it, and under it too, which can be reached when the tide is low. There are grottoes and arches and bridges cut out or built up of the soft stone, and doubtless, when the place is full of a gay and smartly-dressed company, it must be very attractive. You see it is the border land of France and Spain, and you read in the street announcements almost as much of one language as of the other. I should think, however, that with the destruction of the empire a great deal of the *prestige* of Biarritz must have fled, and that it is never again likely to see the *éclat* which distinguished it when the Franco-Spanish Empress made it her temporary home.

I intend leaving here to-morrow morning, and hope to be at *Pamplona* in Spain by night, but I can learn little of the movement of the trains, and shall have to pick up my knowledge as I go on.

LETTER V.

AT BIARRITZ.

GENERAL ASPECT OF BIARRITZ—VILLA EUGÉNIE—
BARENESS OF TREES.

Biarritz;
March 11, 1872.

I DID not intend that you should have another letter from Biarritz, but when I rose this morning the sun was shining so beautifully that I determined to give myself another day before entering upon my long journey. I do not think though I should have done so, had it not been for my troublesome leg, which the cold and damp have not improved. I considered that walking about in the sunshine instead of sitting the whole day in a railway train would be more likely to do it good, and so I have remained, making a closer acquaintance with Biarritz, inhaling the now light breeze from the Bay of Biscay, baking myself in the sun, and cogitating over my proximate Spanish campaign.

I think as regards this little town I know it thoroughly, for, although its aspect would of course be much changed by a brilliant company, the features of the place must be the same. It is certainly pretty, but of course, just at present, rather dull, for there are very few of its not numerous shops open, and the announcement we have often joked about, *à louer*, figures upon two thirds of its houses. Some of these notices, indeed—like the "Apartments" at the west end of London—are painted up *en permanence;* these are somewhat larger buildings, but the majority are tiny *boxes*, in which a family of three or four would literally have to be packed, and, judging from the little attention to "sanitary matters" in this part of the world, I should not much fancy one of these close lodgings in the height of the season. The houses, like those in the environs of Torquay, are built here, there, and everywhere, but Torquay, to my mind, is beyond all compare superior to Biarritz. I look in vain here for trees; there is nothing but scrub, and the want of shade must make it frightfully hot in summer. But it must be a *vrai Paradis* to the French and Spaniards who care little or not at all for fine natural scenery, delicious turf, and well-laid-out gardens, with perfect comfort and propriety *within* doors. They would find here music, society, dress, play, intrigue, gaiety, and parade. What more can French or Spanish men and women require to make them happy?

The Villa Eugénie is a fine, square building of red brick and stone, placed on a gentle eminence facing the sea, and just without the town. But it looks terribly *bare*—the only trees being some poor stunted pines, which have been enclosed to make a park, and are surrounded by an *oaken* fence, *painted green*. A chapel, with gilded eagles for capitals to the columns of the portico, stands at the entrance of the grounds and might contain perhaps fifty people. Every entrance to the place is now placarded with the words, " Propriété Nationale," and during the late war the villa itself was turned into a hospital. I did not care to go inside it, but learned from a communicative *facteur*, whom I interrogated, that it had been restored to something like order, and was exhibited to the curious.

In its neighbourhood there are two or three other villas of some pretension to architectural beauty, and more are building. The style of these new houses is superior. The little town evidently sprung up in the first instance "all in a hurry." Some of the streets appear to lead nowhere except round the corner, and many contain about half a dozen houses, all of which appear *à louer*, and precious little hovels some of them must be.

I am lodged at the Hôtel d'Angleterre on the Place *Sainte* Eugénie. On the height behind the hotel, my landlord, a very worthy fellow, is building a splendid "caravanserai" commanding an extensive view of the Bay.

The warmth of the sun, now it *does* shine, convinces me that I am in the south—a fact further revealed to me by seeing two Englishmen bathing in the open; not a wise thing, by-the-bye, as the wind is still fresh. Vegetation, I find, where I can see it, for there is not much visible, is more advanced than I supposed. The lilacs are out in full blossom. The oleanders are flourishing in the open air, and the weeping willows are in leaf. But, I repeat, there is very little vegetation to be seen. The storms to which this coast must be liable, exposed as it is to the Bay of Biscay, would destroy all trees, and in fact, Biarritz and its neighbourhood are even more nude of them than Brighton, for at least the Pavilion Garden has some good specimens, and beautiful ones are to be found at Preston, on the one hand and Portslade on the other.

On the whole, then, you will gather that I am not *enthusiastic* in praise of Biarritz, although I am quite willing to admit its quiet and secluded situation, and that full advantage appears to have been taken of its capabilities.

LETTER VI.

BIARRITZ TO BURGOS.

ENTRANCE INTO SPAIN—FIRST APPEARANCE OF THE COUNTRY—SPADE HUSBANDRY—TROUBLESOME EXAMINATION OF LUGGAGE—MIRANDA—ARRIVAL AT BURGOS—A SPANISH FONDA—SPANISH BEGGARS—THE CATHEDRAL—SPANISH HOUSES—PUBLIC PROMENADE.

Burgos;
March 13, 1872.

IN accordance with the information I gave you in the envelope of the letter I posted at Biarritz yesterday, I started for Spain by the Paris train which passes the little station at one o'clock.

A short run brought us to the frontier town, Irun, where the joint ceremonies of the examination of passports and overhauling of luggage were duly gone through. It took an hour to complete them, although I must say they were not very rigorously performed.

Here I had to make the first use of my Spanish, as the officials did not speak French. Not being able to book myself or my luggage through to Pamplona, I had to take a fresh ticket at Irun, which again they would only deliver me to Alsasua—the junction for Pamplona—where we were timed to arrive at five o'clock. As. however, I found that I should have a good hour and a half to wait there, I did not much trouble about the matter, but resumed my place when the train was ready to move on.

You may imagine that as long as daylight lasted I kept my eyes wide open to catch everything interesting on the road. The land-locked bay of Pasages, and the height of San Sebastian formed pretty pictures as we slowly passed them by, and the country subsequently traversed by the line looked peaceful and pastoral. The sheep grazing on the scanty pasture were small but snowy white, with beautiful long wool, and the lambs were charming. The houses had in my eyes a very Italian look—that is, Italian of a second or third rate order, and one or two villas that we passed were very like some of the country houses in Piedmont.

The pass of the Pyrenees also greatly resembles part of the road from Bologna to Pistoja, there being a couple of dozen tunnels and one or two bold viaducts, whence were obtained some fine views into deep valleys, there is, however, no such grand panorama as that of the Val d'Arno with Pistoja nestled in the plain, nor are there any chesnut or walnut forests such as we are accustomed to in the Apennines. There are some imposing mountains with square tops on the left, in the direction of Navarre, and one or two of the more distant were covered with snow. But the passage of the Pyrenees, at the point selected by the railway, cannot for a moment compare with any of the passes of the Alps from Switzerland into Italy.

On descending towards Alsasua the few trees hitherto observable had almost disappeared, and every lateral branch of those that remained had been lopped away. The husbandmen in this part of the world have a horror of every thing that will produce a shade, which they consider prejudicial to their crops, and their very vines are cut down to within a foot or so of the ground. How unlike the system prevalent in Lombardy! where every species of vegetable product flourishes, and where the vines, trained in festoons from tree to tree—the very trees themselves, the mulberry, being productive— are succeeded by crops of every description: wheat, Indian corn, hemp, flax, rice. Here in Northern Spain, the monotony after a time becomes painful, nor can the eye rest, as it does throughout Italy, upon picturesque old towers, perched like eagles' nests on the top of every commanding height! The houses, where visible, are as I have mentioned, somewhat similar in character to those of Italy, but there is no attempt to trail the vine, as in the latter country, over trellis, or terrace, —a custom which gives such a charmingly romantic air to most of the Italian villas.

I observed some specimens of the Spanish spade husbandry, which appears excessively laborious and must be very inefficient in a country like this, for the spade never penetrating beyond the same depth must naturally render the sub-soil as hard as flint and but little fitted to receive the roots of tender plants. Three labourers (whereof two were generally women) drove their pointed spades into the ground in a row, and then, at a signal all raised the sod together. The result was a very irregular furrow, and I should say that a plough of even the simplest construction would do the work better in a third of the time. This, however, I leave to be decided by those better acquainted with such matters than myself.

On reaching Alsasua I learnt, to my annoyance, that there would be no train for Pamplona till one o'clock the next day. It was then five in the afternoon. Now, Alsasua is a village without a commonly decent inn, and those who know anything of Spain will not feel surprised at my experiencing a little alarm at the idea of perhaps sleeping in an outhouse and going almost without food for twenty hours. Making, then, the best use of my time, I succeeded in getting a ticket for Burgos, and as it was too late to have my trunk re-registered I persuaded the guard to let it be put back in the luggage van and allow me to settle for its carriage on arriving at my fresh destination. This he did very courteously and I managed to get all through before the train started.

It was not the fault, however, of some over-zealous custom-house officials that I was not left behind after all, for whilst I was getting my ticket, my belongings stood in the middle of the platform, and being espied by the said gentlemen in authority, who were lounging about muffled in their cloaks and smoking cigarettes, they insisted upon my unstrapping my portmanteau, that they might see what it contained. I vainly explained that it had been examined at the frontier. They had made up their minds to investigate its contents, so, with as good a grace as I could command—the guards vociferating meanwhile " *Señores Viajeros al trén,*" tantamount to our " Gentlemen take your places,"—I hastily undid the fastenings and throwing open the trunk gratified the curiosity of the officials and that of a score of idlers who had gathered round us. The search was confined to a dirty hand being thrust through my clean linen, which it simply rumpled and soiled by the operation, after which I was blandly told that I might shut up again. This I did very willingly, and the chief guard having considerately stopped the train till my luggage was put into the van, I jumped into the first carriage where there was room and we were once again in motion.

In the compartment in which I now found myself there were three other passengers, and, curiously enough, we all four represented distinct nationalities—a Frenchman, a Spaniard, a Hungarian, and myself, an Englishman. The Spaniard, a Señor F—, happened to be known to me, and like his two fellow-travellers, he was on his road from Paris to Madrid. He told me that I was visiting Spain at a time when a great deal of agitation was likely to prevail, owing to the approaching general elections, and he seemed to take an ultra-gloomy view of the young King's prospects. I happened to inquire whether the king was making progress in the language. "I believe so," was his reply, "but I much doubt whether he will remain long enough to finish his education."

Night now came on. We got out at Miranda (the junction for Zaragoza) where I made my first acquaintance with a Spanish *mesa redonda* or *table d'hôte*. The food was tolerably abundant, but the meat tough, and fish was served in the middle of the dinner. After a cigar and little more chat following upon the resumption of our journey, my companions, who were entering on their second night, went to sleep, in which blissful state I left them on my arrival at Burgos at ten o'clock.

I was glad to find an omnibus outside the station to convey me to my hotel, the "Fonda del Norte." But what an omnibus! Its patched windows had surely never been cleaned since they were put into their miserable, paintless, make-shift frames, and the body of the vehicle was on a par with its covering. It gave me a foretaste of the place to which I was bound, and wisely prevented my expectations being too highly raised.

After entering the town, which was in darkness, and rattling over some very uneven stones, the omnibus pulled up at a door where a dirty stone staircase led up into the house. On reaching the landing I found a couple of black-eyed, slatternly wenches, who being summoned by a loud call from the driver, were prepared to show me my room, the door of which was opened by a key as large as two of our ordinary street door keys welded into one. As I anticipated, the chamber was in unison with the omnibus and attendants, containing merely a bed on an iron frame, two worm-eaten chairs, a dirty console and a dirtier commode, all of walnut, and precisely of the kind we are accustomed to in Italy, without the marble top, and many, many shades cloudier. The brick floor was, however, covered with a carpet made of odds and ends, put together without any regard to pattern, but as the night was very cold there loomed upon me the chance of escape from the misery of the live-stock, with which, I am sure, the place was well inhabited.

Having walked about the room for a good half hour, one of the aforesaid maids brought me the linen which she assured me, in answer to my inquiries, was *seco y limpio*, well aired and clean. It certainly was white, and having passed a night between the sheets I have every reason to believe they were dry. Any way, poor as the accommodation was, I felt thankful at having escaped Alsasua.

I was awakened once or twice in the night by the *velador* or watchman calling the hour, as our own used to do in the days of my childhood, accompanying his cry, as the "Charlies" did of old, with information about the weather. It says something in favour of Spanish nights, that he is so accustomed to vociferate *sereno* at the end of his monotonous cry as to have obtained that designation as a nick-name. The sound, the appearance of all around me, and the "internal economy," of which I had had a glimpse, were wonderfully suggestive, and drove my memory back two score of years at least.

After getting some breakfast I lighted a cigar and strolled into the streets, but had only got as far as an open *Espolon*, or esplanade, by the river Arlanzon, than I was marked out as fair prey by several most importunate beggars, who, wrapt in their patchwork cloaks, made of every variety of brown cloth, stiff with dirt and grease, but with one end cast majestically over the left shoulder, followed me about and gave me not a moment's peace while attempting to examine some wonderfully heavy statues and a couple of fountains with which the *plaza* was intended to be adorned. One ragged imp, about twelve years of age, pursued me for upwards of an hour, and even followed me into the cathedral, where he stood and stared at me whilst I listened to the service. He got nothing, however, for his pains beyond, perhaps, satisfying an ardent curiosity.

The cathedral, made familiar to me by engravings, and more especially by Roberts's beautiful picture, is certainly a magnificent gothic structure. It reminded me in its external appearance somewhat of the Church of St. Ouen at Rouen, though, of course, having in its favour all the venerableness due to its six centuries of age. Grand as the interior is, and splendidly as the light is disposed, it is greatly disfigured by a *coro* and *reja*, or bronze grating; the latter is very massive and elaborate, but both are terribly in the way, as they utterly prevent your taking in the whole, or even great part, of the building at a glance. The church is rich in statuary, principally bas-reliefs, and the *Capilla*, or chapel, *del Condestable* is admirable.

There are no chairs in the cathedral, and the women as they enter the central portion, surrounded by the *reja* referred to, fall directly on their knees upon the *estera*, or matting of the country, which there covers the pavement. The women occupied the centre, the men kept to the sides, and they remained upon their knees or sitting back upon their heels (the females then looking like squat black balls) for a good hour and a half. All wore veils, a kind of bastard mantilla, a few of lace and the rest of some soft woollen manufacture, and being all black, you might have thought you were assisting at a funeral. Mass was followed by a sermon, or rather homily, to which great attention was paid. The congregation, however, must have had better ears than myself if they could make out the whole of the preacher's discourse, for like many ministers in our own country, he had a habit of dropping his voice at the end of each sentence and finishing it off in a mumble.

From the cathedral I turned into the town, examining its houses and peering into its shops. The former have a very Italian air, though few are furnished with *persiane*. Some of the balconies have a neat contrivance, which very much takes my fancy, and which has most probably been borrowed from the Moors. I refer to a species of conservatory built over them, not, indeed, for the reception of plants, but the convenience of the ladies, who are thus suspended over the street and can see all that is going on without being exposed to the air. Some are neatly curtained inside and adorned with rude carving exteriorly, so that they become really pretty objects. The shops, as might be expected, are poor. Spain produces little of herself, but she admires the gewgaws, tinsel, and *articles de fantaisie* of Paris. The windows therefore display a quantity of cheap rubbish and a few of those gaudy and not very decent prints exhibited in the Rue de Rivoli and the *Passages*. There were show-plates of various photographers appended to a dozen doorways, but the models must have been unexceptionally ugly, and the execution was of the commonest.

Dogs seem abundant in the streets, and make them resound with their barking and howling. They are otherwise harmless, which is fortunate, as they are chiefly mongrels of the mastiff breed, and some are very large. Many seem to have no owners, but wander about picking up offal—true Oriental scavengers—and looking wretchedly thin.

Tired of the town, I wandered into the country, and climbing the heights behind the castle, which played a conspicuous part in the Peninsular war in 1812, enjoyed a fine view of the Pyrenees I had quitted capped with snow, and of the city which lay at my feet—the delicately carved spires of the cathedral rising majestically from the mass of houses.

On descending from my "point of 'vantage," where I had been perfectly alone, I struck into the public walk along the banks of the Arlanzon, bordered by poplars. There was a good sprinkling of people, and there were some well-looking ladies, who had nothing, however, special either in feature or dress to distinguish them from the Milanese. One or two bonnets were visible among them, but the veil formed the head-dress of the majority. The men were becloaked to the eyes. It is amusing to see how these Spanish "lords of creation" take care of themselves by covering in triple broad cloth, whilst their women folk have only a lace veil to protect their head and shoulders from the cold.

If you find this letter written somewhat "up and down" please attribute it to the real cause, viz., my want of accommodation. My room does not boast of such an article of furniture as a table, and the *commode* which I am using makes but a poor substitute, more especially as one of the feet or knobs on which it originally stood is missing, and the ill-grained *meuble* tips up just when it is wanted to be most steady.

LETTER VII.

BURGOS TO VALLADOLID.

ASPECT OF THE COUNTRY—COUNTRY TOWNS—VALLA-
DOLID—HOTEL SERVICE—THE MUSEUM—CATHEDRAL
—SILVERSMITHS' SHOPS—THE MARKET PLACE.

Valladolid;
March 14, 1872.

ANOTHER stage upon my journey! I was up this morning at four, and long before daylight was being carried slowly along, a solitary passenger in a first-class compartment, fortunately supplied with hot-water foot-boxes or I should have suffered with the cold.

As soon as the rising sun permitted me to see the road I perceived we were traversing a treeless tract, with roughly cultivated fields, extending to a low range of sandy-coloured hills on either side, which, with scarcely an exception, formed the scenery that met my eye during my five hours' journey. Nothing could well exceed the monotomy of such a scene, and as to the one or two little towns which were visible, such as Villodrigo, Torquemada, Venta de Baños, and others of less note, they looked the very abomination of ugliness and sterility. The bettermost houses are built of such stone as the country affords, and approach so nearly to the colour of the soil that you have much ado to separate them from it. The poorer habitations or rather hovels are composed of mud, and there is not a tree—scarcely a shrub—observable; and as vegetation is not much advanced in this bleak region, there was only occasionally the relief of the young green corn. You do not, as in traversing the Romagna, where the country too is often savage enough, get a glimpse of those fine mountains crowned with an ancient city or fortress. Here you have only flat dun-hued hills, which show neither habitation nor vegetation, and, in fact, where the only objects that break the sameness are a shepherd or two, or perhaps a team of mules, mounted or unmounted as the case may be, conveying solitary travellers or light goods from one village or townlet to another. The sole interest of the journey lay in the loungers and passengers at the various little stations, at each of which we were detained an inordinate length of time. Some of these men looked picturesque enough, and an occasional neatherd with split sheepskin by way of breeches, round hat, sandals, bronzed face, and the eternal cloak, or a striped blanket which did duty for that garment, made a picture of himself.

I find Valladolid in character very similar to Burgos, but much larger, and with somewhat better shops. Owing too, in part most probably, to the presence of the University, there is more life in the streets, and the market is a particularly gay scene, being well provided with vegetables, salads, and green peas. The wonder to me is, where they can have come from.

The *Plaza Mayor* is a fine open square, and there are one or two others of sufficient space. The theatre too has struck me as a

very capacious building viewed, as I was
only able to view it, from the outside. As
there is plenty of granite not so very far off,
this material is extensively used for pillars
and the basements of the larger buildings,
but the houses are for the most part mean,
of one to three stories in height, built of
brick and roughly plastered over. You traverse part of the city under arcades, formed
of square pillars, all alike, and therefore possessing none of the picturesqueness of Padua,
or the mixed quaintness and grandeur of
Bologna. The streets are badly paved, but
most of them are furnished with footpaths,
which is so far a comfort. The shops as at
Burgos display only the commonest articles,
but they are chiefly of French origin, but
occasionally some familiar English trademark affixed to a box of comestibles or an
article of wearing attire will give you a
friendly wink of recognition as you pass.

My hotel is the "Fonda del Siglo" or of
the *century*, a grand designation indeed, but
I do not pretend to guess the age referred to,
whether the 19th or the 16th. It is a supe-

rior house to the "Norte" at Burgos in respect of fittings and accommodation, but inferior in one particular—that of attendance. At Burgos we were waited upon at table by two very willing if not overclean damsels, and a niece of the landlady, a bright black-eyed girl, who spoke French very tolerably, having spent some time at Angoulême. Here, at Valladolid, the only attendants are two unkempt and slovenly boys, one about sixteen the other fourteen, who give you your bread with their dirty fingers, and pitch rather than place your plate, knife, and fork before you when they need changing.

I must remark too of these northern Fondas (my own limited experience being fortified by that of older Spanish travellers whom I met at table) that there is no one to receive you on your arrival but the porter below, and on proceeding up-stairs, the basement floor being generally a storehouse, you have a room assigned to you as if by favour, and get little or no attention when inside it. God help you! if alone and you are taken ill. Few things I should dread so much as any serious malady in the Peninsula. On the other hand, the Fonda of the north is not expensive. You get a cup of coffee or chocolate and two hearty meals a day, breakfast or luncheon at 11 or 12 and dinner at 6, have no " service " or *bougies* put down to you in the bill, and pay from thirty to forty reals per diem (six to eight shillings). This of course includes the wine, which by-the-bye is not much to my taste, being dark and heavy, and tending rather to the *port* than to the *Bordeaux* flavour.

The museum here contains a few tolerable pictures and specimens of sculpture. Its most curious objects are, however, the painted and gilded wood sculptures taken from suppressed and ruined convents, which, however good they may have appeared in their right places, give you a notion when beheld here of a collection of huge dolls, only fitted for the nursery of Brobdignagian infants.

The cathedral is in strong contrast to that of Burgos, which, as I have mentioned, is gothic, with all the beautiful tracery peculiar to that style of architecture. The church at Valladolid is, on the contrary, square and classical, and at the first glance reminded me of Sta Rosalia at Palermo, though four centuries younger than that remarkable edifice.

It is the work of Herrera, the architect of the Escorial, and has the grandeur and defects of that master's style. It is blocked up interiorly by an immense *reja*, and further disfigured by a huge wall of masonry, so that you have no chance of taking in the interior as a whole. This, however, is not the architect's work and is more to be regretted as the proportions of the building are evidently very fine.

Valladolid possesses, like Genoa and Florence, a street of gold- and silver- smiths', or, rather, the latter, for silver-plate is alone visible. Some of the designs are quaint and many are very elegant, but the workmanship appeared to me to want finish. I was struck with a table ornament for salt and pepper. The two little cellars were in the conventional shape of a human heart, the upper parts or covers of which were transfixed by arrows, from which a chain led to the centre handle; by twisting this the chains tightened and the lids of the cellars were raised.

In the market-place I caught sight, for the first time, of the pig-skins used for the conveyance of wine. They were lying in the sun like actual porkers *sans* bristles, head, and trotters, but retaining in their bloated condition a sufficient resemblance to the real hog to make the look of them unpleasant. One of these unsightly carcases stood beside my portmanteau at the station at Burgos, and on my inquiring, as I pressed my finger on it, whether it contained wine,—seeing it to be stained with what I took to be the generous liquid,—its owner answered "*No, Señor, es Sangre.*" It was *blood!*

LETTER VIII.

VALLADOLID TO MADRID.

STERILE SCENERY—A STONY TRACT—LARGE OLIVE TREES —VIEW OF THE ESCORIAL—ARRIVAL AT MADRID.

Madrid;
March 16, 1872.

I QUITTED Valladolid yesterday at the same hour as I reached it the morning before, at 9 a.m., and on entering the carriage I had to contemplate nearly twelve mortal hours before I could arrive at Madrid.

If you wish to see the country through which you are passing—a not unnatural feeling for an inquisitive traveller who visits new scenes for the first time—you have no alternative but to take the luggage train to which passenger carriages are attached, and the rate of speed from first to last is about ten miles an hour. The faster trains, misnamed *Express*, only run at night.

And what a picture of nakedness it was

which I did behold during the twelve hours of daylight! After leaving Valladolid some distance behind, we came upon a forest of stone pines, not the tall graceful trees beloved of Turner and Harding, and introduced into their Italian landscapes, but stunted things with cauliflower heads, looking, in fact, like some gigantic, sickly vegetable. Then followed scores of miles of a treeless tract of a dirty brown, but without one blade of grass or other green thing in the fields (for though there were no hedges, walls, or ditches, to divide them it was evident that they were separate plots) which were grubbed up rather than prepared for the crops, and occasionally there appeared some black stumps pruned down to within a few inches of the soil, which were presumably vines; but how unlike those of Lombardy or Tuscany!

The few villages discernible were scarcely fit for human habitation. But for the steeple of the church rising in the midst, the eye might pass over the cluster of houses unobservant, as they had no verdure near them, and were the exact colour of the soil from which they sprang. Where a bank allowed of it, the peasantry had burrowed into it like rabbits, and then closed the entrance with a door.

We stopped for refreshment at the station of Avila, and as this same city is the capital of its province—has played no mean part in early Spanish history—has two or three churches and a Gothic cathedral dating back to 1107, and seems to have been strongly fortified for the date of its construction, I expected to find a very different place. Ford says, "its distant appearance is imposing;" perhaps, as that same distance "lends enchantment to the view," I was *not far enough off*, or it may look different from the *carriage* to what it does from the *rail* road. It seems old enough to belong to the early ages of mankind, but the dusky colour of the granite of which it is built, the sterile look of the country in the neighbourhood, and the slimy banks of the River Adaja, by which it is watered, render it a forbidding-looking place.

On quitting it we came upon a tract, the like of which I only remember in the commencement of the descent of the Splügen on the Italian side. A region of granite boulders of the most extraordinary size and character. Monsters of every shape appeared there. Huge toads, sea-horses, vast slugs, and those antediluvian animals with which modern science has made us acquainted, were presented to my wondering gaze in turn, watching in grim, eternal silence the passage of the snorting engine. Busts of men in armour, sleeping giants, and other incongruous shapes were not wanting. Up or down, before and behind, there was nothing but granite stones; and great, indeed, must have been the labour and expense which attended the driving of the iron road through such a perverse and desolate region. As the men employed upon the line could find no villages where to lodge during their ungenial toil, temporary houses had to be erected for them along the line, and the removal of the timber (that valuable commodity in this country) as they went on, by creating a

4

constant succession of ruins, contributed not a little to increase the desolation of this region.

These stones were succeeded by a forest of olives, which did not look the *youngest* production of that ungracious soil, so gnarled and hard appeared their trunks that one could not help fancying the granite had entered into their composition, and that an axe laid to their roots would blunt as though struck upon veritable rock.

More stones and more olives—then the two mixed up together in one scene of confusion, with the distant mountains soaring beyond, covered with snow.

The enormous pile of the Escorial came in sight as the evening was falling—perhaps the most favorable time to observe it—as the reddish stone of which it is built was brightened by the rays of the setting sun. It stands at the top of an eminence, and is backed by the sierra. It looks a huge barrack, having, they say, 11,000 windows, with a dome in the centre.

Although but twenty miles from Madrid, it

took our train two hours and a half to perform the journey, and it was therefore quite dark when I reached the capital.

The confusion at the terminus occasioned by touters, porters, omnibus drivers, cabmen and idlers, was something startling, accustomed as I have been to such scenes for years. I got into a poor little omnibus at last, marked " Servicio Publico," and desired the driver to convey me to the Hotel Peninsulares.

What a drive that was! Whether the man was impatient at having waited so long, with such a small result as a single passenger with a solitary portmanteau, I cannot say, but he covered the ground from the station to the city at a hand gallop, and I found myself, owing to the wretched nature of the road, flying between my seat and the roof every few seconds, while clouds of dust made all outward objects indistinguishable.

Whether true or not, a man who stood at the door of the "Peninsulares" told me there was no room, but conducted me to a house opposite. It turned out to be a " Casa de

Huespedes," or private boarding establishment, kept by a lady and her two daughters. I was shown into a neat little carpeted *gabinete*, or sitting-room, with a terrace looking on to the street, the Alcalá, the principal *calle* of Madrid, close to the *Puerta del Sol*, and having an *Alcoba* attached, in which was the bed, separated from the *gabinete* by glass doors. It looked, as I have found it, very clean and comfortable, and I am glad of the chance which has conducted me hither rather than to the hotel.

A cup of very decent tea, obtained from a neighbouring café, was welcome after the journey and dust, and a good night's rest has quite recovered me from my fatigue.

LETTER IX.

MADRID.

SPANISH COOKERY—GOOD BREAD—FIRST APPEARANCE OF
MADRID—ITS STREETS—SOLDIERS—MILITARY MUSIC.

Calle de Alcalá;
March 16, 1872.

I OPENED my eyes this morning for the first time in Madrid, to salute a bright sun and deliciously blue sky, though I found on getting into the air that it was very keen.

At half-past eight the *mozo*, Faustino, brought me in a cup of *café au lait* with half a roll toasted, but *no butter*. (I have only tasted that comestible *once* since I left France, and have felt no inclination to try it again.) The breakfast hour is half-past eleven. Dinner is served at half-past six. Breakfast consists of eggs fried or boiled, or an omelette; then chopped kidneys or something analogous; a piece of meat with potatoes; cheese, fruit, and wine. Dinner is composed of soup, kidney beans, or *garbanzas* (chickpeas), and two meats served one after the other, the atter with salad; some sweet cake or preserve, cheese, and fruit.

The meat is tough, stringy, and tasteless, and the oil in which the things are fried is green and very rank, so that when cooking it is enough to turn a delicate stomach; garlic enters largely into the flavouring, and altogether the food is coarse, greasy, and little nourishing. The bread and water are both good. The Spanish *wheaten* bread is perhaps a little *too close*, somewhat like our aërated, but it is deliciously white. French bread (*pán francés*) is most in use, and is very light and agreeable. The wine is not to my taste, being flat and inclining to sweetness. It is supposed to be from *Valdepeñas*, but as that district has a reputation, one may take for granted that " it knoweth not such origin."

The windows of my *gabinete* open on to a balcony nearly opposite the Custom House, an imposing building of red brick, with stone facings. On my left hand is the " Puerta del Sol," that favourite lounging place of idlers,

and to the right I look down towards the
"prado" which, on reaching the bottom of
the street, stretches to the right and left.
The *calle* itself rises and then dips considerably towards the public walk. Indeed, few of
the streets of Madrid are on the level, as the
city is built on several sand hills, and, with
the exception of some half-dozen main
thoroughfares, the *calles* wind and twist
considerably. They are almost all provided
with foot-paths, but the road pavement of
the older portion of the town is composed of
flints, and is very trying to your feet and
patience when driven off the narrow footways, a common occurrence enough, as the
Spaniards, I perceive, give room to no one,
male or female.

The Alcalá, a fine street enough, is to
my mind disfigured by a double line of tram-
way, or *tramvia* as they have translated it.
Distances are not so great in Madrid that
ordinary omnibuses would not have answered
the purpose, and the "Calle de Alcalá" is
not broad enough for this mode of conveyance. Everything has naturally to make

way for the huge omnibus of the line, and when the troops are passing up and down the streets they have to turn aside and break the order of their march, which greatly destroys the martial effect.

A propos of these same soldiers. The infantry (fine stalwart fellows on the whole) when marching out to parade wear, for the most part, no boots, but a leather sole fastened on with sandals or thongs (the true ancient Roman foot-covering), and as many dispense with stockings, their dirty toes give them a slovenly look, rather out of character with the rest of their attire. The uniform is composed of a blue loose coat, red or blue trousers with red stripe—very wide and baggy—black gaiters, the aforesaid "sandalled shoon," and white or green gloves. Their drums and trumpets are neither pleasant nor musical. Noisy they are, for the first perform a continual rub-a-dub, and the latter are sounded often without the least reference to the band behind, and whose music is completely destroyed by the discordant accompaniment.

LETTER X.

MADRID.

A MISSING LETTER — SPANISH POST-OFFICE AND ITS OFFICIALS — CIGARETTE-SMOKING — MADRID HOUSES — PUERTA DEL SOL — SPANISH WOMEN — CASAS DE HUESPEDES.

Calle de Alcalá ;
March 17, 1872.

I POSTED you a letter last night and should have sent you this to-day, but that wishing to write a few lines to A. and J. I put it off till too late, as the post leaves early here. However, this will start to-morrow and you will be the gainer by getting a longer letter.

I made particular inquiries at the postoffice this morning about your missing letter, for I am *sure* you have written to me. They are so obtuse here and so *insouciants* that I feel convinced the missing epistle is lying in some pigeon hole to which it does not belong, owing to their not understanding your E in my name. I begged the officials to look under G and Ll. This, after a little demur, they did, without success in the instance at which I required it, that is to say *your* letter, but it brought to light one from W., which their perspicuity had also failed to understand. If I am able to give you another address whilst in Spain I will ask you to print your E thus, **E,** so that there can be no possibility of a mistake.

The scene enacted at the post-office window during these enquiries was so Spanish that I cannot refrain from describing it to you. Knowing that the officials and I should not agree about the *pronunciation* of my name, I exhibited my passport and asked if they had letters for the person therein described. A clerk, who was leaning against a table, doing nothing, leisurely took the credentials, and having examined them and mumbled the name over to himself, suddenly remembered that he had not had a cigarette for the previous ten minutes. Whereupon, lying down the document, in which " We, Lord John Russell, request and require, in the name of Her Majesty, that A. E— may be afforded every assistance, &c., of which he may stand in need," the worthy *empleado*, from one pocket drew his roll of papers, and from another his tobacco pouch, and having carefully rolled up the desired delicacy, with fingers dyed of a deep saffron colour from constant occupation of the same kind, he took from a third pocket a box of wax matches, the lid of which was ornamented with a not too decent representation of a French *lorette*, and having expended two in procuring a light, for the head of the first rolled off when applied to the sandpaper, he blew through his nostrils two streams of smoke, much to his gratification and, doubtless, to the clearing of his faculties. This done, he condescended to re-examine my passport, and having again listened to my humble request, he proceeded, with that gravity which became a Spaniard, to do the little work for which he was placed there and, I presume, paid for to perform.

I am now in a position to give you some

notion of what I think of Madrid, having spent a couple of days in walking about its streets and attentively examining every object that has come in my way.

It is certainly a fine city being, in parts, very regularly built, with some grand palaces and public buildings. These have very much the appearance of Italian ones, granite taking the place of marble. The majority of them, however, are of brick covered with *compo*, only the compo is harder than with us, and does not peel off with the alternations of the weather. Here, as in Burgos and Valladolid, the glazed terraces are not uncommon, and some of them being tastily covered outside and neatly curtained within, not only have a pretty appearance but form admirable nooks whence to observe the passers by. But all said, Madrid has a very modern aspect; there are not many vestiges of antiquity about it; one looks, of course, in vain for any traces of the Moor who has left such graceful and indelible marks of his presence in other parts of the Peninsula and the seal of age does not appear to be specially impressed on any edifice or monument. This may be in part due to the atmosphere, for the *Plaza Mayor* is upwards of two centuries old.

I am in the Calle de Alcalá, the finest street in Madrid, which, like the Corso at Milan, leads to the principal drives and walks. Fortunately, my bed is placed in an *alcoba* or recess, shut in with glass doors, otherwise the noises of this noisiest of thoroughfares and *latest* of cities would be as unpleasant as the Corso, just mentioned, on one occasion proved to you. I am also close to the Puerta del Sol, which is not a gate as its name would imply (there *was* one there originally), but a rather fine *Plaza* or " Squarr," as the French have it, into which eight large streets debouch, whereof the Alcalá is one.

This Puerta del Sol, as you know by repute, is the favourite lounge. It has always a sunny and a shady side, it has some good shops, and there, from the passion of the Spaniards of all classes for lounging, all sorts of costumes and all sorts of people may be studied in it. The Puerta del Sol has been famous during the thousand and one revolutions that Spain has gone through, and if one might judge from the aspect of a great part of its *habitués* there are plenty of elements for a rising at any given moment.

The cloak which Spaniards of every degree seem so fond of gives them a sinister air. Even when the sun shines brightly they wrap themselves in this *capa* to the very eyes, and there is no doubt that in many instances it is used to hide the little more than nakedness beneath. The beggar's cloak is a thing to behold. Made of so many patches that it is hard to determine of what material the original garment was composed, the end of it is yet thrown jauntily over one shoulder, and it is very evident that the constant asking of alms has not diminished the self-esteem of the wearer. Peasantry of various districts are always found too lounging in the Puerta del Sol. Some of their hats are wonderful; round, turned up at the brim, and furnished with two or three tufts or puffs of floss silk or wool. Braided and velvet jackets are also common, with breeches and gaiters. Many wear no shoes, but in their place *soles* of pigskin fastened to the feet by thongs of leather.

The women have a very Italian look, and a very *Milanese* look among Italians. The eyes are perhaps finer, and I think, on the whole, the *Madrileñas* are better looking. I certainly have seen not a few fine women in the Prado. They get very stout after a certain age, and whether they wear "dress improvers" or not, or whether nature has been *specially* bountiful to them, I cannot say, but their proportions are *large*. A great many, indeed most of them, still wear the mantilla, and a few the high comb; but, however Spanish the latter may be, the veil looks more graceful without it, more particularly with the present fashion of dressing the hair.

I believe I told you I am not in an hotel, but in one of the numerous *Casas de Huespedes* or boarding-houses. The family consists of the father (a nonentity), the mother and mistress of the establishment, a stout, kind, old soul, and two daughters, who have beautiful eyes, and are otherwise good-looking enough if they would only be a little more particular about their attire, and Faustino, a big, long-legged, but very good-natured fellow, is the *mozo* or waiter and general chamber-*man*. The inmates are a Spanish colonel, a Peruvian, two brothers, Spanish merchants from Barcelona, and myself. With the exception of the brothers, who know a little French, they speak no language but their own, and I am compelled to exercise my Spanish. I would advise all who wish to derive pleasure and profit from a journey through Spain to get up some knowledge of the language, for in scarcely any European country will the traveller find so few who are capable of holding converse in any tongue but that with which they are born.

Their proficiency in English may be estimated by an announcement which appears in large letters over a first-class restaurant in the Calle de Alcalá, where one reads with bewilderment that "Dinners" are served "by the *cart*."

LETTER XI.

MADRID.

THE MUSEUM OF PICTURES—THE SPANISH SCHOOL—
VELASQUEZ—MURILLO—RIBERA—JUANES—COELLO—
ZURBARAN—SPECIMENS OF THE ITALIAN SCHOOL.

Calle de Alcalá;
March 17, 1872.

I WROTE you a few lines from Bordeaux, and as L. tells me you have seen most of the intermediate letters I need not go over the old ground. You know that I have reached this capital, the *only* court, if we are to take the Madrileños' dictum as gospel, "*Solo Madrid es corte,*" and I propose this evening to give you a brief account of the Museum of pictures in which I have spent some few hours.

It contains an immense number of works, more than 2000, and of course an infinite deal of spoiled canvas. On the other hand, it has treasures beyond all price, and some beautiful specimens of the Italian and Flemish schools.

I was struck at once by the works of three men of whose labours I had hitherto seen but few examplars, Velasquez, Murillo, and Ribera. The first is a grand and masculine painter. Every canvas to which he put his vigorous hand seems to live and breathe. Whether portraying the Don or his Jester, the Señora or her Dwarf, he is equally in earnest, and never before had I conceived how great was his power. On a close examination his colours seem to have been literally thrown upon the canvas, as if he wielded his brush like a sword and slashed at his work, but the effect, when viewed at a little distance, is truly marvellous. There is a Christ crucified, with the partly-clotted hair hanging over the drooped head, that makes you shudder, so wonderful is its execution, so terribly like unto death. Murillo, on the other hand, is sweet, delicate, and fascinating. His women are delicious, but his Madonnas after all are but lovely amiable-looking women,

> " . . . . . not too bright and good
> For human nature's daily food."

They want that indescribable divinity which distinguishes Raphael (whom, by-the-bye, Valasquez could never appreciate). *His* Madonnas, indeed, seem made to be *worshipped*, Murillo's to be *loved*. Murillo's flesh colour and draperies are charming, and one marvels where in this country he could have obtained his models, for their type is very northern. Of course, I have not yet seen many Andalusian women, and when I visit Seville, Murillo's native place, I may find there the counterpart of his Madonnas. There is a fine picture of his in the long gallery on the right, styled a Holy Family, but it is no more *holy* in character than any innocent domestic interior can be so designated, where a man and woman in the prime of life are watching with loving eyes the awakening intelligence of their first-born.

Ribera, known in Italy as *lo Spagnoletto*, wields a grandly vigorous pencil, but his subjects are simply detestable. Hermits reduced to the last stage of emaciation, martyrs suffering under torture, blood, and dissection, these are the themes in which he delights, but, although admitting his power, I for my part incline to that naughty Don Juan's doctrine, and prefer turning from—

> . . . "Saints and martyrs hairy,
> To the sweet pictures of the Virgin Mary."

There are some delightful pictures by Juan Juanes, called the Spanish Raphael. They are certainly Italian in manner, but are nearer in style to Pietro Perugino, Raphael's master, having a stiffness and hardness from which Raphael was wholly free. Some of his heads, though, are beautiful; their colouring is all that could be desired—whilst others are pure caricatures. Witness the caput of Judas Iscariot in the Last Supper, with its flaming red hair, hooked nose, cunning eyes, and generally diabolical expression. That man could surely never have wormed himself into the confidence of any one except an idiot. It is decidedly a *portrait charge*.

The gallery has also several specimens of another Spanish artist, hitherto unknown to me except by name, Zurbaran; and until I came here, I must confess myself to have been lamentably ignorant of the works of Sanchez and Claudio Coello, both fine painters.

The Italian School is well represented, though the chief pictures are by Venetian masters. There is a replica in the long gallery of that splendid Danäe of Titian, one of the glories of the Museum at Naples, but the Madrid exemplar is in an unfinished state. At a little distance higher up there are two large pictures by the same master, which are puzzling. They represent in almost identical positions, and with the same background—a garden—a young man playing on a spinnet, with his face turned towards the naked figure of a woman lying on a silken couch behind him. In the first of these pictures the woman, whose model has evidently been the same as that of the two celebrated Venuses in the Tribune at Florence, and who is depicted with all the charm of colour proper to Titian, is toying with a little dog; in the second she is listening to the whispers of a prettily little cupid. At the first glance I thought I saw in this change of playmate the effect of the gentleman's harmony, converting playfulness into love; but, to the destruction of my theory, I afterwards perceived that the man was older and bearded in the "dog" picture, and a mere youth, a perfect *blanc bec*, in the other, though evidently intended for the same individual; the woman being in both cases of the same age. I could find no one to enlighten me on the subject, and the catalogues are discreetly silent.

The gallery contains two magnificent Raphaels; one, the celebrated "Perla," originally the property of our Charles the First, and purchased of Cromwell for Philip IV, who exclaimed at sight of it—" This is the *pearl* of all my pictures,"—hence its name. The other is the equally celebrated

Agnus Dei, which has suffered at the hands of restorers. I noticed also an old acquaintance of Velasquez, *Los Borrachos,* of which there is a replica much esteemed and copied in the Gallery at Naples, representing a group of peasants carousing, one half-drunken fellow being covered with vine leaves, by a companion. It has all the manly vigour noticeable in the works of that great master.

LETTER XII.

MADRID.

A DREARY EVENING—THE OPERA HOUSE OF MADRID—KING AMADEO—THE PRADO—PASEO DE LOS RECOLLETOS—THE WET-NURSES OF MADRID.

Calle de Alcalá;
March 19, 1872.

PLEASED as I am to write to you, knowing with what satisfaction you will read the lines I trace; it is a very one-sided kind of pleasure, as I can get no acknowledgment in return.

Never, perhaps, have I felt a separation from all my dear friends so severely as the present. No doubt part of this arises from my feeling less at home in Spain than in Italy. With the latter country I have been familiar from my childhood, but here, indeed, I feel alone. I sent you a long letter yesterday, written on Sunday evening, but it is very difficult to do anything by the light of two miserable attenuated candles, and with pale ink. Last night, therefore, I was obliged to give up this generally effectual cure for my loneliness, as I naturally feel less solitary when jotting down notes which I know will reach your hands and be read by your eyes.

At dinner there were only the Colonel and myself, and he was under marching orders for Murcia. After he had gone Doña Maria, my landlady, and her two daughters kept me company during dessert, and we talked *tant bien que mal*, but rather *mal* than otherwise, at least on my part, about various matters. I showed them your portrait in my locket, which they declared in loud terms to be *muy guapita*. At last I retired to my room, took my coffee and a cigar, and read for an hour. I then, as I mentioned, tried to write, but, owing to the miserable "illumination," gave it up in despair. Ennuyéed beyond bearing, I seized my hat—it was then 9 o'clock—and went into the bustling street, chance, rather than design, leading me in the direction of the Opera House. I procured a ticket for a *butaca* or *fauteuil* and went in.

A second-rate Italian company were in the middle of the first act of L'Africaine, the said Africaine being quite ugly enough for her part without the paint. She did not sing very well, but she showed quite sufficient *passion* for the copper complexion she wore. The tenor was good, the rest as usual, were so so. The house, which is at the side of the Plaza del Oriente, and close to the royal Palace, is a very fine one; I should say nearly as large as Covent Garden. There is no pit, properly so called, the whole of the area being occupied by stalls or *butacas* of red velvet and very comfortable. My ticket cost me only eight francs. Rather different to London opera prices. There was very little, indeed *no* beauty, that I saw. The mantilla was universal, and, with very few exceptions, the ladies wore high-necked dresses. The Spanish ladies, I understand, are not partial to the display of their—necks. There were three, however, quite uncovered enough in a box above me, one having the entire edge of her dress lined or bordered rather with artificial flowers, which gave her the appearance of a variegated Clyte. The Royal box is placed, as in Italy, in the centre of the house.

By-the-bye, talking of royalty, I saw from my balcony yesterday afternoon the young King Amadeo ride down the Alcalá with a general officer on each side of him, and followed by a couple of footmen in scarlet livery, and a few dozen lancers.

It was painful to me to observe the dead silence which attended his progress. The street was crowded, yet not a single "viva" did I hear. "No man," as York says of Richard, "cried God save him." Nay, scarcely a hat was raised, although it struck me that the young king sedulously looked about in order to acknowledge by a military salute the *nonchalant* way in which some few *touched* their hats as he passed.

I cannot but sincerely pity his position amid this pompous, empty, and restless people. His fate may not be so tragical as that of Maximilian, but he is amongst a cognate race, and if any outbreak do occur, he may esteem himself lucky if he escape from Spain with life. "*Mais que diable allait-il faire dans cette galère?*" as Molière makes Géronte exclaim. He certainly would have better consulted his own happiness by stopping at home. But then, I suppose, these sons and daughters of monarchs are just as anxious to obtain kingdoms of their own as a merchant's son is to enter into business on his own account.

The king was followed by Her Majesty, his royal spouse, who, judging from her face, is a woman resolved to hold her own as long as possible. It is a determined, even a haughty countenance, though not wanting in a certain dark beauty, but a strong contrast to her sister-in-law, the sweet Princess Marguerite.

I have not yet spoken to you of the public promenades which are always well frequented in the afternoon, and most interesting to a curious stranger, from the contrasts they present. The "Paseo de Recolletos" in the Prado is at the present time the most fashionable resort, and the authorities have done what they could, by the planting of shrubs to make it attractive. The result, in the way of shade, is nothing to boast of, but in an arid climate like Madrid one gets thankful for very small mercies in the shape of verdure. In process of time this particular walk will be much improved, for it is being bordered by fine houses and detached and semi-detached villas—quite a new feature in this part of the world.

At the entrance is a marble statue of Cybele seated in a car drawn by two horses, water spouting from beneath their feet into a capacious basin. The execution is bold, but the result of the whole is unsatisfactory, the seated figure looking far too squat for dignity. There is a corresponding fountain representing Neptune at the end of the Salon, or the opposite part of the Prado which faces the museum, and another of Apollo, not wanting in grace, stands between the two.

There are several *paseos*, or promenades, scattered about Madrid, all of which are similar in character, being bordered by stunted trees, and require to be well-watered to keep down the dust. At the "Recolletos," the road for carriages runs between two broad footways, and there is also a narrow slip for horseriders, likewise bordered by footways. There were a few, say half a dozen, young ladies on horseback when I visited the paseo yesterday, and perhaps a couple of dozen cavaliers; but the space is so confined that accidents must often occur through reckless riding. I myself saw one young fellow on a restive horse come into collision with another and fly out of his saddle with more expedition than grace. He wasn't hurt, however, only sandied, and his horse being stopped by a young officer, he was able to remount and continue his way. The carriages were greater in number and far better horsed than I could have thought possible, judging from the population of the city. Many of the ladies in them were bareheaded, if women in this age of chignons and elaborate coiffures can be so called; many others wore the mantilla, and the minority were in bonnets. This same rule, as regards headdress, held also among the promenaders, where occasionally the high Spanish comb was visible.

Beyond the mantilla, there was nothing to distinguish them in dress from the ladies of London or Paris. The gowns were just as long, and, as a consequence, on returning from the promenade they were disfigured with the dust which they swept up on their way. Black silks were most numerous, but there were some maroon, one or two vivid green, which is not inharmonious with their complexions and eyes, and one orange colour.

The men were as three to one lady. They all looked well dressed, but without anything distinguishable. Occasionally one met a *majo* dandy, with well-made black trousers, short, well-fitting velvet jacket, ornamental waistcoat, and round wool cap, but he was the exception.

I must not, however, omit to mention the wet-nurses, who, like those of Paris and the Italian cities, appear in gorgeous array. Those of Madrid are generally peasant women from the Asturias. They wear a white cap, with a short gown, often of cerise colour, trimmed with gold or silver lace, and a white embroidered apron. They are brave in trinkets, and some of their ear pendants and brooches are curious specimens of old-fashioned jewellery.

LETTER XIII.

MADRID.

THE MANZANARES—LAUNDRESSES OF MADRID—BRIDGES—
—MULES AND DONKEYS — DOGS— BEGGARS — THEIR
GUITARS—THE LOTTERY.

Calle de Alcalá ;
March 20, 1872.

I HAVE traversed this city in every direction, and think I know its features tolerably well. Every one who comes to Madrid is attracted first to the " Puerta del Sol," where in former days there stood a gate, hence its name of *Puerta,* and which constituted originally one of the limits of the city. It is now a spacious *place,* in the very centre of the town. It has a fountain in the middle, and some good buildings and shops round it, the chief hotels being above them. The principal streets radiate from this *plaza*, and it is therefore always full of life and motion. As there is one side always sunny while the other is in the shade, crowds of idlers bask there, *al sol* in winter and spring time, and *á la sombra* in summer.

Go when you will into the "Puerta del Sol," you are sure to see many of the same faces, as if their owners lived there, and, so far as concerns the greater part of their lives, they most probably do, rolling up cigarettes and smoking them at their leisure all day long.

This cigarette-smoking must be an enormous resource for these idlers, as time is naturally "killed," as they themselves style it, in the preparation and consumption of these dainties. I wonder if any Spanish statistician has ever calculated how many valuable hours of their lives are expended in this way!

I walked down to the Manzanares in order to see the great washing-ground of the Madrid laundresses. It is a curious sight. The muddy banks are literally lined with women engaged in their occupation; the stream being diverted into several narrow channels for greater convenience. Thousands of garments were hanging in the sun, and the gabble of many women and the melancholy songs of others (for they sing as constantly and much in the same style as the peasantry of Italy) filled the air.

The Manzanares is crossed by three or four bridges. Two of those I visited, the Toledo and the Segovia, are of vast proportions, quite out of character with the miserable stream; but then they deserve just as much the name of viaducts as bridges, for most of their arches are dry.

The Royal Palace looks very fine from this part of the town, and it is, indeed, one of the grandest buildings in Europe.

In the poorer localities I traversed to reach the great washing-ground above described, I found much more life and character as there are situated many inferior hostelries (*posadas* and *ventas*), where the peasantry of the surrounding districts put up, and about the entrances of which they crowd. The women are undistinguishable from the Neapolitans of the same class, going bare-headed, or wearing a silk handkerchief over the back of the head. Fair or light-brown hair is by no means uncommon; in fact, I saw more fair women than I have usually seen in France.

Mules and donkeys (the latter much larger than with us) perform most of the labour allotted elsewhere to the horse and cart. They carry everything upon their backs, from water to paving-stones. Their owners disfigure the poor creatures to the eye by cutting off all the hair of the upper part of their bodies—I could not learn whether to prevent vermin or make them more impressionable to the stick—and the skin is black and tanned, as if it were already converted into leather. Indeed, so evenly is the hair removed that I thought, at first, each beast was covered with a leather cloth. When these animals are very thin, as is most frequently the case, and exhibit their poor ribs to view, the sight of the carcase is most unpleasant; and when the stick falls upon the bare back or sides (which alas ! it too often does) the sound is like the beating of a carpet.

Dogs, a species of mongrel mastiff, abound in Madrid as, in fact, in every town of the Peninsula I have yet visited. As they are constantly thrusting their noses into the heaps of rubbish collected in the streets and their prominent ribs show that they would not be particular about their food, they must serve, in some degree, as public scavengers. They seem very quarrelsome among themselves and are snarling and fighting great part of the day and night, but no one seems to pay the slightest attention to them, except to bestow a kick upon some lanky carcase to make it move out of the way.

Water being one of the great necessities in all countries, and more particularly in Spain, this valuable article is sold about the streets and at every railway station by regular vendors—*aguaderos* or *aguaderas*, for they are most commonly women—and the cry of *Agua, Agua! Quien quiere agua?* is one of the commonest that salutes the traveller's ear. In the "prado" and along the Calle de Alcalá leading to it, these water-sellers abound, and judging from my observation, the quantity consumed must be considerable.

The beggars of Madrid have attracted a good deal of my notice from the fact of their being so unlike those of any other city. They are almost all blind and almost all, male and female, are furnished with a guitar. Not that they play or seem capable of playing any tune on it. They simply strum, strum, strum, and twang, twang, twang, across the strings, with or without the accompaniment of the voice in nasal, dolorous accents. One stout, blind fellow, with this eternal instrument in his hand had fastened a string round the waist of a dirty little imp of six or seven years old, who thus led his progenitor or master like a dog. The sturdy fellow, meanwhile, as he ping-pinged, followed his small leader and puffed away at a cigarette which lolled out of the corner of his mouth. In fact, like their betters, these mendicants are constantly smoking, and are becloaked in the same style.

I find the Lottery, sanctioned by Government, as great an institution here as in Italy, and there are as many offices for the sale of tickets as there are *estancos* or licensed tobacconists. It is true the prices of the tickets are not so low as in the country just mentioned, but, on the other hand, as they are divisible into fractions it comes virtually to the same thing.

LETTER XIV.

MADRID.

VARIATIONS OF ATMOSPHERE—UMBRELLAS—A WANDER ROUND THE CITY—DOS DE MAYO—PLAZA MAYOR.

> Calle de Alcalá;
> *March* 23, 1872.

THE weather up to yesterday had been uninterruptedly clear and bright from the moment of my setting foot in Madrid. The sun was hot, but the wind remained still keen, and no wonder, for although this capital is as far south as Naples, it is 2000 feet higher, and the Guadarrama chain of mountains, visible from different parts of the city, is covered with snow. Still, the heat was sufficiently great to compel the soldiers to put on their puggeries, and very pretty they looked when marching in a body.

But yesterday a change came over the atmosphere. The wind blew in gusts; rain clouds shut out the sun, so that it turned very cold, while perfect *tourbillons* of dust made the air misty.

To-day the same menacing clouds have melted into rain, which has continued to pour down for many successive hours.

The umbrellas it has brought to light are marvellous to behold; they differ in size from an ordinary dinner-plate to a small tent, and their colours are as various as the tints of the rainbow. We Northerners, with our sober notions and liking for blacks and browns, can form a poor conception of the taste which a Spaniard displays in this useful article, the *paraguas*. The hues of his umbrellas, run through every gradation of colour, from yellow to green, from blue to indigo, from pink to the richest maroon. I saw some like a huge golden pippin or melon cut in two. I observed others of a hue as deep as the pomegranate blossom or damask rose, and, in fact, as I gazed upon them from the height of my terrace, I thought I beheld a *parterre* of flowers or a collection of circular leaves, whose colours ranged from the fresh green of spring to the autumnal tints upon the Virginian creeper.

As soon as the rain a little abated I put on my thickest paletôt, for it was bitterly cold, and turned into the streets, which were, of course, nearly deserted.

The cabs here are furnished with a little tin flag bearing the inscription "*se alquila*" (for hire), which is raised when empty and depressed when engaged. The idea was borrowed, you may remember, in London a year or two ago, but, as usual with us, not being strictly enforced, it has, like the cabmen's tickets, fallen into disuse. The Madrid coachmen evidently think this printed announcement a sufficient indication of their being at your service, for they seldom or ever ask if you need a coach, but doze upon their boxes or make and smoke cigarrettes till they are hailed. On this particular afternoon, however, one actually, seeing me plodding through the mud, did inquire whether I wanted a conveyance, but as I had no notion where I was going to, I declined the proffered service.

Chance led my footsteps to the prado, and in the opposite direction to the "Recolletos," or fashionable promenade. Passing by the gate of the gardens of *El Buen Retiro*, that have been closed during the whole time of my stay here, I traversed the Salon del Prado, and having passed the Museum, which occupies one side of it, came upon an obelisk enclosed within an iron railing, whereon appeared the simple inscription, *Dos de Mayo*.

The words recal one of those sanguinary episodes which hideously mark the presence of Napoleon's troops in Spain. General Dausmenil, acting under the orders of Murat on that fatal 2nd of May, put to the sword unnumbered groups of old and young, not even sparing the clergy, and this monument is intended to hold up the memory of that ruthless chief to the execration of posterity.

Passing up the Calle de Atocha I at length reached the Plaza Mayor, the most regular and one of the most interesting squares in Madrid. It was here, as we may read, that the *Autos-de-Fé* were celebrated, and on state occasions bull-fights were held in the Plaza, for which the locality is well fitted. Philip IV here entertained our Charles I to one of these spectacles, and as recently as 1833 a grand entertainment of the kind was given on the inauguration of Queen Isabel, when it is stated that nearly one hundred bulls were converted into beef.

If the weather improve I propose making a trip to-morrow to the Escorial, as on Monday I start for Saragossa and the towns on the east coast. As next week is the *Semana Santa* I expect to find more play than work going on. The streets of Madrid are placarded with the notices of excursion trains to Seville, whither half the world of Spain seems flitting, and where, as usual on such occasions, a fine harvest is being garnered by the hotels and other places of public lodgment.

If I am not too tired to-morrow night I shall have the pleasure of giving you my impressions of the Escorial, a building as abused by some as it is belauded by others, and which the majority agree in dubbing one of the " Wonders of the World."

LETTER XV.

MADRID.

A TRIP TO THE ESCORIAL — THE APPROACH FROM
MADRID — ENORMOUS EXTENT — STRANGE DESIGN —
THE CHAPEL — THE PANTHEON.

Calle de Alcalá;
March 24, 1872.

IN common I suppose with a good many others of my fellow-creatures, I had formed the most erroneous notions of the situation and character of El Escorial.

In the first place, before I came to Spain I was under the impression that it was in the immediate neighbourhood of Madrid instead of being twenty miles away (*two hours by rail*), and secondly, I had conceived the idea of its being half palace, half museum, whilst it is much more of a monastery and a mausoleum than either of the former, as Philip II, for whom it was built, must be considered as living the life of a monk rather than a monarch, and the edifice was ostensibly raised for a royal burial-place.

I have already spoken to you of the utter barrenness of the country which so painfully affected me on approaching the monstrous pile from the north. Darkness came upon me after leaving it behind on my journey from Valladolid to Madrid, so that when this morning I started for the spot with the huge building for my destination, I had some curiosity to gratify.

Better would it have been, perhaps, if the darkness which then enveloped the country still continued to cover it, for my fancy might have turned some of the desert into smiling landscape and peopled the two or three intermediate villages with a gay and pleasant population. As it was, the full light of day was thrown upon the arid stony tract and the begrimed and gloomy-looking people, and the result upon the spirits became depressing in the extreme.

You will say this was not a very proper frame of mind in which to visit and estimate the vast monument I had come out to see, but yet somehow the two seemed to be in harmony with each other. I was about to behold one of the gloomiest of piles, and I arrived at the station from whence it becomes clearly visible in as melancholy a condition as if I were to become one of its inmates.

It stands upon lofty ground, and has an attempt at green shrubs and stunted trees about its base. A little village is huddled beneath its walls, the houses of which look all the smaller from the enormous size of the building which overshadows them. A bare, desolate sierra rises behind it, and far as the eye can reach—north, south, east and west it alights upon the same dun-coloured soil, streamless, treeless, hedgeless, with nothing but some scattered stones to break the monotonous surface.

Your whole attention is therefore soon rivetted upon the vast granite pile before you. You wonder how it could have stood, roasted by the suns of summer, and beaten by the snows and tempests of winter, for more than 300 years, and yet look so fresh and new.

Its strength must be enormous, or it could not have stood such trials as it has done, but it looks as if it were intended to stand a siege, and its vast size and the smallness and bareness of its countless windows give it the appearance of a barrack.

Built by two of Spain's best architects, Juan Bautista de Toledo and Juan de Herrera, it was dedicated to St. Lawrence, and in further honour of that saint its ground plan is that of a gridiron, whilst the saint himself, represented in stone upon one of the portals, is roasting in all due form, somewhat after the fashion sculptured over the chief entrance to the cathedral at Genoa.

It would be quite beyond the limits of a letter to attempt a description of a building which has been described as "at once a temple, palace, treasury, tomb-house, and museum," and about which many volumes have been written. The guide who conducted myself and others through its vast courts and cloisters so bewildered my head with details, which he gabbled through as long as he had breath, that I cannot for the life of me remember whether he said there were 3000 staircases and eighty feet of fresco painting, or the reverse, but as the reading of those numbers the other way would seem to be more correct, I suppose they should be taken in a different order to what I have put them. I saw for myself that there were sixteen different *patios*, or courts, and that the fountains—some of which were playing—were very numerous.

There is a chapel in the centre of the huge building surmounted by a cupola, the proportions of which are beautiful and harmonious. It is rich in marbles, and the frescoed roofs by Italian artists are very effective. The most striking objects are kneeling effigies in bronze gilt of Charles V, Philip II, and many female members of their families. These are well worth careful study, but the guide allows you but short time for their examination; and the light, too, as usual, is too scanty and broken to allow you to judge of the pictures by a dumb Spanish artist, Juan Fernandez Navarrete, surnamed on account of his infliction *El Mudo*, which are described by Ford as "magnificent .... possessing the bravura of Rubens, without his coarseness, and with a richness of colour often rivalling even Titian." How he could manage to see all this is more than I can divine; *my* sight is none of the weakest, and I tried very hard to examine them properly. The subjects are in harmony with the place, being full-length figures of saints and apostles.

The "Pantheon," strange name for a *Christian* place of burial, is situated beneath the high altar. You descend to it by a staircase lined with jasper, and on reaching the bottom you find yourself in an octagon-shaped vault, adorned with costly marbles and gilded bronze. The sides are hollowed into niches, containing black marble urns, which are actually filled with the remains of Spanish royalty, whose names and titles are indicated by appropriate inscriptions. The polished marbles, and rather profuse gilding, seen by the light of the wax tapers carried by the guide and visitors, make a magnificent show, but the feelings of reverence which the abode of death naturally excites, and the reflections which *such* a place, in connexion with *such* names, are apt to engender, are smothered as soon as formed in company of such a guide, and when bored by the presence of a dozen sightseers of the character with which my lot happened to be cast. I would have given something to be permitted to turn them all out, the guide more especially, and spend half an hour in the place alone.

I should extend my letter to too great a length if I attempted to describe the cloisters or *patios*—some of them with fish-ponds— the library, the kitchen and numerous *salas* spread about the building, most of which were visited in turn till brain and legs got tired out together. And yet there were few or no pictures on the walls, and but few *movable* artistical productions. Some of the former have found their way to the Museum at Madrid, others were removed to France, and have never been returned, whilst La Houssaye and others, either moved by a *love of art*, or, as his detractors say, a fondness for the precious metals, carried off everything he could lay his hands on in the shape of silver and gold, and thus unwittingly read the Spaniards a lesson out of the very books which had served for the instruction of Cortes, Pizarro, and a numerous band of followers.

This trip to the Escorial has occupied me the day, and has left an impression on my mind of a monstrous waste of masonry and splendour. How such a building is to be kept up, at so great a distance from the capital, and with an exchequer so impoverished as that of Spain, and what use it can possibly be put to, are questions which will somehow force themselves upon the mind. They did not, however, so trouble mine as to prevent me going fast asleep as soon as the train on its return journey was lazily put in motion, and it was in such a blissful state of forgetfulness that I was conveyed almost to the terminus at Madrid.

LETTER XVI.

MADRID TO SARAGOSSA.

THE ROAD TO SARAGOSSA—ANCIENT CITIES—ALCALÁ DE HENARES—GUADALAJARA—THE HENARES CANAL—SIGÜENZA COVERED WITH SNOW—THE MOORS—CALATAYUD—ARRIVAL AT SARAGOSSA—AN OLD ACQUAINTANCE.

Fonda de las Cuatro Naciones, Saragossa ;
March 26, 1872.

I HOPE you received my last letter from Madrid detailing my visit to the Escorial, and wherein I told you I would write again on Tuesday. I reached here safely, but somewhat tired, last night, after fourteen hours' railway travelling.

It is a dreary tract of road you have to traverse, and in the present instance it was a cold ride. On leaving Madrid the line rises considerably, and on either side you behold the same treeless space, with sand or limestone hills and flat tops, which have nothing to render them pleasant to the eye.

The traveller's interest is first awakened by the appearance of the old city of Alcalá de Henares, formerly boasting a university and still looking imposing, with its high, square buildings and church spires.

Two stations further on he will observe Guadalajara, which, placed upon the river Henares, is not wanting in picturesqueness, although the absence of trees and the abundance of stones make the picture a desolate one.

A few miles in advance the line crosses the Henares Canal, the work of an English company (the "Iberian Irrigation"), which has an air of solidity and finish about it, unusual in modern works in this part of the world.

As the road runs on, the aspect of the country becomes more and more desolate. Rocks, with occasional enormous olive trees, were followed by comparatively level ground, which produced nothing but stones. Not a scrap of green was observable for miles together; and to make the aspect still drearier, I perceived—as I expected from the recent rains at Madrid—that the soil was covered with patches of snow. At length a region of snowy crags was reached, without any evidence whatsoever of vegetation or habitable dwellings.

The roofs of the ancient city of Sigüenza were white with snow. Climbing up the hill, in the form of an amphitheatre, the old town had an air of rude grandeur, with the *Alcazar*, half fortress, half palace, on the summit. A fine aqueduct crosses a glen on the left of the city as viewed from the railway, and lends additional picturesqueness to a really fine landscape.

As the train approached the border-land of Castille and Aragon, ruins of old castles were occasionally visible. This was the great battle-ground of the Moor and the Spaniard, till the former was worsted, and retired to his last stronghold—Granada.

On entering the ancient kingdom of Aragon at Ariza there was a change for the better. I had got out of the snow region, and although the savage features of the landscape—the torn rock, the beetling crag, and the rushing, turbid torrent—were still there, they were interspersed with little, smiling valleys, where the corn was green and where flourished hundreds of pear trees, looking wonderfully refreshing with their multitudinous blossoms. Vegetation, however, throughout every part of Spain I have yet visited, is less advanced than it was at Biarritz a fortnight ago. And yet I am as far south as Rome.

Calatayud cannot fail to attract the traveller's attention, not only because the train stops there for the purposes of refreshment, but because he finds time to look about him and admire the old Moorish city propped up, as it were, with rocks, and furnished with what appears to be a grand castle.

From this point I noted a succession of vines, trimmed down to the black knotted stumps, and interspersed with olive trees and crags. The temperature became milder. The snow had disappeared, and in the neighbourhood of some of the little towns, such as Mores and Morata, there were green vegetables to refresh the eye after the universal duns, greys and browns of the landscape.

Saragossa, or to adopt the Spanish spelling Zaragoza, was reached a little before nine. What a scene of confusion! What a babble of words, issuing from the throats of touters for the *Fondas* and *Casas de Huespedes*, and from the travellers themselves in furious contention with porters and mendicants! Fortunately I discovered the omnibus of the "Cuatro Naciones," the hotel I had selected, and in which I took refuge, as a man would do from a swarm of hornets, and left the conductor to battle out the question of my luggage.

I have been fortunate in the selection of my hostelry. I have a simple, but comfortable and airy room overlooking the "Calle de Don Jaime 1°," one of the principal streets; and this morning I had the greater reason to congratulate myself on my choice, as, when seated at breakfast, there came into the room a tall, white-mustachioed gentleman, whose acquaintance I had casually made at Biarritz. Colonel P—, who had served in the Spanish army as well as in that of his own country, France, immediately recognised me, and came to take his seat by my side.

Being well acquainted with the city he volunteered to act as my cicerone, an offer with which I gladly closed, for it is very different to have as a companion an educated and intelligent gentleman to marching along with a *valet de place*, or wandering about alone, which has been my fate hitherto.

I must reserve for another letter the result of my observations as the dinner bell is ringing, and my sheet is already full.   Adiós.

LETTER XVII.

SARAGOSSA.

ASPECT OF THE STREETS—ANCIENT HOUSES—EL COSO—
THE CASINO—THE ALJAFERIA—TWO CATHEDRALS—
THE EBRO—SPANISH MARKETS.

Fonda de las Cuatro Naciones, Saragossa;
March 26, 1872.

It is now 11 p.m., but as I leave to-morrow for Pamplona I write you a few more lines to be posted in the morning.

In company of Colonel P——, I have devoted some hours to walking about the city; I could not very well have ridden, for there are no vehicles plying for hire in the town, and the majority of the streets are fitted neither in dimensions nor paving for coach exercise.

The peculiarity of Saragossa lies in the remains of its former greatness, and its half Moorish, half mediæval Christian character.

The older houses and streets are purely Moorish, the former being squat and solid, the latter as narrow as the narrowest of old Genoa and just as tortuous. But the palaces of the former *grands seigneurs* are now reduced to the vilest uses. I was much struck with one, known as the " Casa de la Infanta," in the Calle de· San Pedro, at present used as a *remise*. The *patio* or open court has some beautifully fluted and carved pillars and brackets supporting an upper gallery, with a frieze containing representations of the labours of Hercules. The cornices above are wonderfully rich and beautiful, and efforts have been successfully made to prevent this fine specimen of Aragonese architecture from going to decay.

Most of the better class of houses, the mansions of the old nobility, are distinguished by projecting roofs with handsome soffits and carved jutting rafters; and, as many of these mansions are built of stone, they have an air of great solidity, which they must in fact possess judging from the date of their erection.

The longest, most regular, and most important street of Saragossa is the "Calle del Coso," corresponding to the "Corso" of Rome and other Italian cities. Striking out of it at right angles is a handsome square, the "Plaza de la Constitucion," planted with young trees, and ornamented with stone seats, a fountain, a statue, and terra-cotta vases. There are a couple of good cafés under an arcade at the side of the square; one of them, the "Iberia," being indeed handsomely decorated.

The Colonel took me into the principal casino or club, and kindly had my name enrolled as a visitor for such time as I might remain in the city. It is held in one of the old palaces I have referred to, and has some good and spacious rooms. The chief salon contains some well-executed portraits (life size) of the kings of Aragon, and a few Spanish celebrities, Goya, the artist, amongst others. The reading-room is but poorly supplied with papers, but that is not to be wondered at in a country like Spain; there are one or two French journals from which, as the experienced know, but little real information is obtainable, and I observed that England was represented by the 'Illustrated London News.' Pictures, and especially such excellent ones as are afforded by the periodical in question, are always intelligible, and from its pages I gleaned certain items of news which I sought in vain in the foreign prints. The rooms are very simply furnished, and the walls of one or two are " decorated " with the most ordinary French coloured lithographs. Convenience for card-playing is observable in many baize-covered tables, and as usual the men smoke everywhere.

Having spent an hour in endeavouring to gather from the papers above alluded to some intelligence as to what the outer world was doing, we resumed our peregrinations, and bent our steps in the direction of the ancient citadel of the *Aljaferia*, situated just without the Portillo gate on the banks of the Ebro.

Originally built by the Moors for the purpose of a fortress, it is used at the present day for the same object, and two regiments of infantry are now quartered there. It happened that my conductor was an acquaintance of the colonel in command, and having been directed to his quarters we were very warmly received. Colonel A— was obliging enough to take us all over the place, and afforded us an opportunity of hearing some spirited music from a terrace overlooking the patio where the band was stationed, a terrace, by-the-bye, that must have been trodden by the old Moorish governors, and afterwards by Ferdinand and Isabella nearly four centuries before our time.

The place is full of interest to the archæologist. At every turn you come upon some little bit of architecture reminding you of the past. A portion of the Moorish mosque, exceedingly minute, but very beautiful in its decay, greatly interested me. I observed more than one door on which a Moorish handicraftsman had been employed, and last, not least, the sergeant who accompanied us with the keys unlocked the door which gave entrance to the splendid "Salon de Sa. Isabel," in which the Queen of Hungary is said to have been born in 1271, that is to say, 600 years ago! The roof is glorious in its wood carving and rich colouring of blue and gold.

On taking leave of our kind host, with many professions of esteem, Colonel P— conducted me to the door of one of the cathedrals, for Saragossa has two, and with a promise of meeting again at dinner he left me to pursue my further sight-seeing alone. I first entered "El Pilar," so called because it contains the *identical pillar* upon which *the* Mary, worshipped in this city, descended from Heaven. The church is under repair, as it has been I understand any time these fifty years. Exteriorly it is a huge, square, ugly building, having various stumpy domes, some covered with parti-coloured tiles; whilst the interior, so far as it can be observed, is classical and unsatisfactory, looking as modern and theatrical as the Madeleine at Paris. The other, "La Seo," or cathedral church *par excellence*, is a remarkable edifice, with such a profusion of carving and bas-reliefs as literally to weary the eye. Fortunately the effect is, in part, subdued by the darkness which reigns there, for the architecture being gothic, the windows are of the smallest, and admit only that " dim religious light" so dear to some, so cavilled at by others.

The Ebro rushes rapidly past the city, and is crossed, just between the two cathedrals, by a stone bridge of vast dimensions, having seven arches. As you stand upon it and contemplate the town with its delicate octagonal towers, very Moorish in style, the place promises more than it performs for it is evidently a dull and dreary residence.

The market seems well supplied with vegetables, and should always be visited by the traveller, as he will see more character and costume in an hour among the cabbages than he will behold elsewhere in a day.

I will write you next from Pamplona, for which place I must leave by daybreak, there being actually but *one* through train between Saragossa and that city in the twenty-four hours.

LETTER XVIII.

PAMPLONA.

DIFFICULTIES OF SPANISH TRAVEL—THE *REAL* INTEREST OF SPAIN—PAMPLONA—FINE SITUATION AND PICTURESQUENESS—TUDELA—TAFALLA—OLITE—BEAUTIFUL MOORISH RUIN.

Fonda de Europa, Pamplona;
March 28, 1872.

BEHOLD me now at Pamplona, the capital of Navarre, and much nearer to France than I have recently been, for this city is quite in the north of Spain, and looks on the map but a stone's throw from Biarritz. But what a throw it would be! The Pyrenees lie between, and they can only be crossed at the extreme points, for civilisation has not carved out for itself the pleasant and romantic roads across this stony barrier which it has done over, and now *through*, the Alps. The roads would not *pay* even if they were made, for I doubt if, amid any of the revolutions of time,

Spain will be visited as favoured Italy. The country is too savage (at least, as regards its northern moiety), the climate too trying, the food and lodging are too poor and makeshift, the people too stiff and unamiable for holiday-seekers. Added to these serious drawbacks, the distances between the towns, where a delicately nurtured traveller can put up, are so very great, and the railway travelling is so slow (rarely faster, indeed, than our old stage-coach) that one gets fatigued to sickness before the journey's end is reached, because there is nothing *outside* to raise the spirits or engage the mind.

I have now traversed Spain from the French frontier at Bayonne to the very centre of the Peninsula at Madrid, and up again to the north-east to Saragossa and Pamplona, and I have found it all the same; for the most part a treeless waste, a dun, sandy soil, or a stony desert. I have discovered little more interest in the aspect of its smaller towns, which approach so nearly to the colour of the ground out of which they barely spring as almost to escape notice, a church spire being the simple landmark which hints at the vicinity of human dwellings.

It is true I have yet to visit the Mediterranean coast line and to run through Andalucia, where I am promised rich vegetation and a world of fresh pictures. I hope it may be so, for if I were to return to England at this moment, having traversed the two Castilles, Aragon and Navarre, I should bring away with me the dreariest memories of Spanish landscape.

The *real* interest of Spain, I take it, lies in the fact of its being *unlike* anything else in Europe; the mingling of much that is African with that which belongs to a *past age* in the rest of our continent. The lower classes certainly approximate more to the Saracen than to the European. The style of dress of both men and women shows this to be the case. The cloak in which the men muffle themselves is nothing but the *burnous*, of different material, and the sandals on their feet are borrowed from the former inhabitants of the Peninsula. The delight, too, which both sexes take in bright colours hints at an

Oriental or African taste, and certainly their manners are far less polished than those we are accustomed to observe as proper to the peoples of other parts of Europe.

During my wanderings I have met with but three lady travellers (I need scarcely say they were *English*). Two of these were strong hearty girls who, with their father, were making their way to England up from Gibraltar. They were not travelling *in* Spain, but merely crossing it to avoid the sea. The other was a lady, with her brother and husband. I met her at the table d'hôte at Valladolid, and of course she could eat nothing that was put before her, but the bread and fruit; for even the fowls are nothing but bone and skin, and that skin is dark and greasy, and, I think, rubbed with garlic.

At the public meals (and bear in mind that you cannot well feed *apart*), I have, with the exceptions I have mentioned, met only *men*, and they smoke in the middle of breakfast or dinner, and clear their throats and spit all over the place in a way that is destruction to a delicate appetite. No wonder that so few ladies come to Spain. It is *not* the place for them. Let them visit France and Switzerland, Germany and Italy, where their wants and requirements are understood and attended to, and where, in beautiful climates and scenery, rich art and gay shops, they can find always something to please their fancy and engage their mind. Here, in Spain—and remember I include Madrid—there is scarce a shop worth looking into. The Peninsula seems to produce nothing of its own. It exhibits only French and English wares, or the meretricious rubbish of the Palais Royal bazaars, *où l'entrée est libre.* Or what it *does* show that is peculiar to itself consists of coarse images of every variety of Virgin Mary, miserable drawings of special saints, or little charms, and trinkets connected with the Church, and they, I fancy, are manufactured at Birmingham or in Germany by the hands of heretics, and are subsequently blessed in a heap to give them the proper virtue and sanctity.

Pamplona pleases me better than any of

the towns of Spain I have yet seen (Madrid excepted). It is a clean, prosperous-looking place with many seignorial houses, as evidenced by the coats of arms over the doorways. Being placed upon a height, it has an imposing appearance, and as the omnibus drags you up from the station you find you are approaching what must have been once a strongly fortified town, whose defences are now entirely in ruins. The views from the deserted battlements are charming. The valley at your feet with the Arga rushing through it, and the mountains beyond with the Pyrenees in the distance, present many fine pictures, and I should say a week might be profitably spent by the artist in this little city.

"La Taconera" is the public promenade. It contains some pleasant, shady walks, where there are actually flowers, whose scent, particularly that of the violets, was quite a new sensation in this part of the world.

Pamplona has a gothic cathedral which is not without interest, though why in the name of good taste the powers that were should have furnished it with a heavy *Corinthian* façade is more than I can divine.

You will have gathered from my general remarks at the commencement of this letter, that the road which conducted me hither did not find more favour in my eyes than those I had hitherto traversed.

The station at Saragossa is on the other side of the Ebro, and as the train left at six I was compelled to be very early astir.

I obtained a good view of the city with the two cathedrals and the delicate spires rising above the houses on steaming out of the station. But I was soon transported into the same sandy and treeless waste I have before described, without apparently any evidence of attempt to utilise the soil.

In the neighbourhood of some of the little towns there is more appearance of cultivation. You occasionally, too, get extensive tracts of olive trees (not a gay plant by any means), and you see the stocks of myriads of vines, not yet in leaf.

The Ebro is crossed twice by long iron bridges, and one or two of the little towns are picturesque. The most notable are Tudela, Tafalla, and Olite, which formed exceptions to the general dreariness of the prospect. The last-mentioned place possesses a beautiful ruin of an extensive Moorish castle, with tall, graceful turrets, looking quite fairy-like, as they rose into the dark blue atmosphere.

The line, also, within a few miles of Pamplona, runs beneath one of the arches of a fine aqueduct, now in use for the conveyance of water to the city.

I start again for Saragossa at three, and shall have seven more weary hours before I can reach it. To-morrow, however, is Good Friday, and I shall be able to get a long rest before continuing my journey to Barcelona.

LETTER XIX.

SARAGOSSA.

GOOD FRIDAY STRICTLY OBSERVED—LEANING TOWER—COSTUME OF COUNTRY PEOPLE—BEGGARS—FRIGHTFUL CRIPPLES—WAITING FOR THE PROCESSION.

Fonda de las Cuatro Naciones, Saragossa;
Good Friday, March 29, 1872.

I WRITE you a few lines to-day to assure you of my safe return from Pamplona. I got back again last night, and although it was near the midnight hour when I reached the hotel, I found my friend Colonel P— at the top of the staircase to welcome me. Really, the French gentleman, of *the old school*, where he takes, is exceptionally kind and courteous.

I fully intended to leave for Barcelona to-morrow, but as I find that owing to the holidays I shall not be able to see certain gentlemen there I am desirous of visiting till after Monday, I have made up my mind to spend Easter Sunday here, with the greater reason as it will give me an opportunity of witnessing a bull-fight, the placards of which have been posted on the city walls for some days past.

This *semana santa*—this "holy week"—is very naturally relished by an indolent people. It is such a capital excuse for doing nothing, to put forward that all work is strictly forbidden. And as far as in them lies the good folks *will* do nothing, and will not allow any one else to labour if they can help it.

They keep this festival of Good Friday very strictly. The colonel and I, tired of wandering about the streets, where a hot wind was raising clouds of dust, an hour ago strolled into the casino to have a game at chess to while away the time. We learned that all the games were *rigoureusement défendus*. The men were lolling about smoking and talking in the various rooms, but the billiard-tables were covered up, the piano was shut, the dominoes were boxed, so we have returned to the hotel, to get up our arrears of correspondence.

During our stroll this morning we came upon a very beautiful leaning tower of octagon shape, built of ornamental brickwork. It is situated in the Plaza San Felipe, and, notwithstanding its apparent insecurity, it has stood more than 350 years. Its base, however, has been considerably strengthened within a recent period.

I am writing this by an open window, which overlooks the street leading to the cathedral, and, as I sit at a short distance from the balcony, the buzz of many voices and the shuffling of many feet reach my ear. The fact is, everybody is out of doors. All they do is to wander about and talk. The spectacle, however, is varied and interesting from the diversity of costume. Some of the peasantry appear in trousers, waistcoat and jacket of black velveteen. A silk handkerchief tied round the forehead, leaving the top of the head bare. The feet protected by sandals, but *no stockings*. Others wear breeches, stockings *without feet to them*, and sandals; the same style of head-dress, and a striped blanket in lieu of cloak cast over one shoulder. The most noticeable article of attire is a sash or rather shawl, red or magenta in colour, wound many times about the waist and covering the stomach. This serves as a pocket for knife, purse, tobacco, and cigarette papers, in fact, it is a general receptacle.

The beggars literally *swarm*, and cripples of every kind thrust their terrible deformities before you, as they used to do in Italy five-and-twenty years ago. There is one lad of fourteen or fifteen who really turns me sick. Nature, instead of hands and feet, has given him claws arranged like the nippers of a lobster. The hands—if they can be so called—he thrusts into your face, to call your attention to his feet. Surely it would have been no sin to suppress him at his birth as a monstrosity.

The dogs, too, are as plentiful, and in one sense are very similar to the beggars. If you give a *cuarto* to the latter, you are pestered to death by the whole tribe, for it is noised throughout their ranks that a charitable stranger is among them. Yesterday, on my way back from Pamplona, I happened to give a wretched lean dog a bone, and immediately after I had six others about me far leaner and more wretched than their predecessor.

I thought that there was more than usual noise and bustle below, and on looking out I find the street is lined with people in expectation of a procession. It will quite take me back to my boyish days in Italy to witness it. I see all the balconies are filled with spectators, and I have discovered that the "maids of Saragossa" are not so bad-looking when in Sunday attire.

I shall go down to Colonel P—'s terrace, for his room is on the first-floor, and therefore but a few feet above the heads of the people, and if the procession be worth recording, I will give you some account of it in my next.

LETTER XX.

SARAGOSSA.

THE EASTER PROCESSION—LAY FIGURES—A COUNTRY DRIVE—IMPOSSIBILITY OF RESIDING AWAY FROM THE CITY—A DESOLATE ESTATE—A PICTURESQUE GUARD.

March 30, 1872.

WHEN closing my letter yesterday I mentioned to you that the people were gathered in expectation of the grand procession which was to pass our hotel. It did so shortly after I despatched that communication, and it was *an hour and a half* defiling past the balcony. I have seen processions galore in Italy, but never did I see such an exhibition as this. It would be too long to give you an account of the order in which it marched past, but I may tell you briefly that the chief incidents of the Saviour's passion, betrayal, capture, tortures, and ultimate death on the cross, were all represented by figures *as large as life*, placed upon stages, and carried by men in the dress of the Misericordia Brotherhood. The figures were of sculptured wood, painted, and you may imagine the size and weight of the "Lord's Supper" when I tell you that it required thirty-two men to carry it. Looking down upon the table, I saw that it was furnished with a wooden lamb or kid in a dish, two drinking vases, and two lanterns; so that unless a miracle were wrought in their behalf, the guests were likely to come poorly off in the way of food and drink.

With these there were Roman soldiers on foot and on horseback, the twelve apostles, Moses, Aaron, Noah, Isaac, Jacob, and many more; the twelve tribes of Israel, the banners indicating them as they passed by; gentlemen and ladies in the habit of the Misericordia, all bearing huge wax candles, and many of the ladies were so blessed with *embonpoint* that their shining, black, calico dresses fitted them *like a glove*. There were rows of young girls dressed in white, with blue sashes and wings, others with red ditto and similar feather appendages. There were gentlemen in dress coats and troops of the peasantry, all, of course, with lighted candles and *gamins* running by their side catching the wax as it guttered and fell. There were bands of military music, and at last, the church proper, represented by priests and acolytes, swinging censers, and all chanting through their noses. There were banner bearers, with pictures of favorite saints and martyrs, and a regiment of infantry to bring up the rear.

There must have been hundreds, if not thousands in the procession. It was more numerous than the spectators who, be it observed, exhibited none of that ultra-enthusiasm which I should have expected from such an exhibition. Hats were only removed by the better class when the Saviour, lying in state on a bed all silver and cloth of gold (as far removed from the *reality* as it is possible to conceive), was carried past.

Altogether it was a wonderful show, and would have been more effective if the procession had not been broken into fragments, owing to the necessity of the bearers, who carried the images, having to set them down for rest every one or two minutes, while those ahead of them shuffled on. This improvised arrangement, however, gave me an opportunity of seeing portions with greater distinctness. The "Lord's Supper," for instance, rested immediately beneath our balcony for a couple of minutes.

This morning Colonel A—, to whom, as I mentioned, I was introduced at the citadel of the *Aljaferia* drove up by appointment to our hotel in a little barouche, to which were harnessed two pretty Pamplona ponies, not much bigger than Shetlands, but most delicately made. He came to convey Colonel P— and myself to a country house and estate, known as the " Torre de T—" (every detached farm-house is a *Torre* (tower) in this ancient kingdom of Aragon), belonging to a friend of the latter, situated about eight miles from Saragossa. This friend had begged Colonel P— to pay the property a visit on the first opportunity, and report upon its condition, as it had been let to a tenant who had decamped without going through the ceremony of paying the rent.

The fields were, many of them, green with corn, and as long as we kept to the high road it was bordered with trees all breaking into leaf. But we soon left the highway for a less frequented track and then the wretched poverty of this part of Spain became visible.

It does not seem possible here to live away from the towns, and, even in them, life, as we understand it further north, is miserable enough; but *in the country*, it is as dreary as if you were in the wilds of Africa or Australia. There are no gentlemen's "seats" whatsoever; nor is this surprising when we reflect that there are no practicable roads.

After some serious "lunges" into the ruts which distinguished the one we were traversing we were compelled to abandon our little carriage before it became a total wreck, and perform the rest of our journey on foot, and that was rather a gymnastical performance.

The "Torre" became visible after we had passed through a wretched hamlet, where scowling men, slatternly women, and imp-like children were lying about the place amid the pigs and poultry. The house stood alone in its own private grounds, surrounded by a mud wall, within which appeared two or three tall cypresses and a splendid stone pine. They were the only green things visible, and as we knocked in vain for entrance at the rude gate I saw that the whole place, the land included, was a complete ruin, the dishonest tenant having abandoned the place after cutting down all the wood he could lay hands on.

We walked round the desolate enclosure, and at length managed to break through a species of hedge into a garden. But what a garden! Some fig trees were there and one or two stumps of vines, with others partly trellised against the wall, but all in utter decay, without the vestige of a flower or shrub, and the ground as hard and white as the road.

On emerging from the broken hedge we saw a figure approaching us, who turned out to be the man (a rural guard) in whose care the premises were left, with his long-barrelled gun slung over his shoulder. What a picture he would have made! His every pose was grace; and whether in his talk, he threw his gun into the hollow of his arm, or reslung it across his shoulder, or pointed with it to any distant object, a native, noble manliness, marked every action.

He wore the usual dark serge breeches with grey stockings, sandals on his feet, a magenta scarf or shawl round his waist, a sheepskin jacket (which at a little distance appeared embroidered, owing to the wearing away of portions of the wool), over which was slung his shooting-belt, and a round, rather high, goat-skin cap. His complexion was mahogany-coloured, and his eyes black and piercing.

Having the key, he volunteered to show us over the house. And what a house! What rooms! Doors of the roughest wood, on which a paint-brush had never been laid; shutters to the windows, but no glass; floors of rude cement as up and down as a ground swell in the Mediterranean, and huge holes in the woodwork where the rats had eaten their way through in search of what it must have been difficult to find—food. A house of the *ninth*, I should have guessed, rather than the *nineteenth* century, and yet people of *blue blood* had lodged there. I could pick out hundreds of labourers' cottages in Kent that would be *palaces* of comfort in comparison.

The estate was on a par with the *mansion*. All had been abandoned and the ground left to run wild. That would mean *in England* being overgrown with rank vegetation, tangled weeds a foot or two high, and green grass everywhere. In Spain it means *the desert*. Not a blade of grass—not a bramble—nothing but grey thistles and colourless stubble, out of which every drop of moisture had been drawn by the scorching sun. In fact, a picture of hopeless desolation.

LETTER XXI.

SARAGOSSA.

A BULL FIGHT.

Saragossa;
Easter Sunday, March 31, 1872.

I HAVE just returned from witnessing a bull-fight and send you a hurried account while the impression is still vivid upon my mind.

As these *corridas* are not of frequent occurrence, they make considerable stir in the cities where they are held, and there is consequently a great rush for tickets. Having procured one in the most favourable place, that is to say, duly in the shade, I found myself, at a quarter to three, one of about eight thousand spectators, among whom were a sprinkling of ladies, a good many women and some children in arms.

The programme informed us there were eight bulls to be killed, a chief *espada* or *matador* and an assistant, three *picadores* and seven *banderilleros*.

The performance commenced by the whole of the actors, including two teams of three mules, marching from the opposite side of the arena to the front of the *palco* or box just above me occupied by the *Alcalde*, or Mayor, and his party.

After a little speechifying, a key, ostensibly *the* key which opened the stall where the bulls were confined, was delivered to the chief spokesman; the party then retired, the ground was cleared of all supernumeraries and helpers, and the mounted *picadores*, who are cased in leather and otherwise well padded, took their place at the side, one of them close by the gate at which the bull was to make his entrance. This done, the gate was thrown open, and the first bull was let out.

He was a splendid roan-coloured beast, and as he dashed into the arena, saluted by shouts from thousands of lungs, he turned about and lashed his tail, seeking for some object on which to wreak his rage. A banner or silk cloak was flaunted within a few feet of him, and on he dashed at it; the *chulo* who held it made for the barrier which he leaped with the utmost agility, the bull driving his horns into the timber only a few inches below the flying foot.

He then espied one of the *picadores* mounted on a grey horse (which, like the others was *blindfolded*). The man received the charge by driving his spear or *garrocha*, which has a point about an inch and a half long, into the bull's neck, and wheeled his horse in the opposite direction. The bull, however, not turned, but maddened by the stroke, caught the right flank of the horse with one of his horns and ripped it open as with a knife, so that the whole of the poor animal's leg was dyed with blood. He was about to renew the attack when a *chulo* interposed with his cloak and induced him to turn in another direction.

The object of the *chulo* or *banderillero* seems to be to constantly call off the bull's attention from any particular attack, and thus tire him out. The *picador* must never attack the bull, but await the beast's assault, and it happens not unfrequently, as I saw it, that the bull, being already familiar with the spear he wields, does not care to renew the acquaintance, but at other times, maddened with the pain caused by his wounds and by his tormentors in the ring, with their blue, pink and orange cloaks, and the hurricane of cries from the spectators, he rushes at the *picador*, and overthrows horse and man. One of these assaults was truly terrific. The bull dashed at the unfortunate horse, drove his horns into the centre of the stomach, lifted horse and man literally off the ground, and then rolled them completely over. I thought there was an end of the *picador*; but the bull being enticed by an interposing scarf to rush off after another adversary, the *picador* was rescued from his uncomfortable position by the attendants and led off to the the side. Not so the poor wretched horse; he was disembowelled, and, notwithstanding the efforts of the helpers to get him up again, seconded by the kicks of their heavy boots and the application of clubs used with no sparing hand, the poor beast simply staggered to his legs and then fell dead.

This same first bull caught also one of the *chulos* when he was waving his scarf, and threw him into the air, so that he fell upon the bull's neck, reeking with his own gore and that of the slain horse, and then slipped to the ground without further damage than the smearing of his silk stockings and orange breeches.

A second and a third horse shared the fate of the first. One was pierced right through the breast, so that the blood poured out as from a fountain, the hole being plugged for the time by a quantity of tow; and the third was caught in the abdomen, from whence his bowels protruded, and in that state he trotted across the arena, amid the shouts and clappings of hands of the spectators.

When the bull will no longer attack the *picadores*, his first fury having subsided and his strength somewhat waning, they retire from the scene, and the ground is left to the *chulos*, who wave the scarf, and certain practised *banderilleros*, with *banderillas* or darts adorned with coloured paper in their hands, who dance about the head of the bull and just as he is about to rush at them stick one of these arrows into each side of his neck, skipping aside with wonderful activity to avoid his attack. Stung with the pain and foaming at the mouth, the animal rushes at every object, and is again received by another pair of the cursed barbs; and when three or four have been thus placed, the bull being nearly exhausted, the *matador*, or as he is called the *espada*, with one or two *chulos* only, appears upon the scene, holding in one hand a scarlet cloth, and in the other a Toledo sword. The bull makes several dashes at the hated colour, but at length stupefied, he stares at it wildly. The *matador* seizes his moment and plunges the bright blade right into his neck behind the horns; and on two occasions which I witnessed, so true was the blow that it was driven up to the hilt and pierced the beast to the heart. He vomited a stream of blood, turned round and round and fell, when, to make assurance doubly sure, an assistant came forward and drove a poignard into the spine.

Shouts, screams of applause, followed; cigars were showered at the matador, who bowed his acknowledgments, whilst in their enthusiasm many cast their hats into the arena.

Then the music struck up. The team—three mules abreast, splendid creatures, covered with *grelôts* and trappings—came in to drag off the slain. A rope being fastened round the neck of the slaughtered animals, they were one by one dragged round the arena, till having reached the opposite side at which they were to make their exit, they were lashed into a furious gallop, and, amid a hurricane of voices in every pitch of excitement and loud cries of *Anda! anda!* they disappeared like lightning. This was repeated with each slain animal in succession, and in the case of the first bull there were three horses killed.

Considerable excitement was caused by the

second—a compactly-made beast, black as night—by his leaping the barrier after the first *chulo* who tormented him. There were about a dozen persons *aficionados*, or keen lovers of the sport, helpers, and others in the narrow passage at the time, but they cleared out in a twinkling, except one, who, being very fat, was not possessed of that ever-ready agility which should be the portion of the man who takes up such a position. He ran for his life, the bull after him, the people clapping their hands and rising up from their seats to see the result, when, the infuriated *toro* bowing his head to clear him from his path, the intended victim made a supreme effort and tumbled over all of a heap into the arena, the bull meanwhile being let through into it by a convenient gate at the end.

The exhibition of slaughter I have above described I saw repeated four times, but finding there was no variation in the sanguinary entertainment except the chance, which nearly occurred, of seeing a man or two killed, I left in a state of tremor and sickness. The main cause of my disgust arose from a poor horse, when disabled, being attacked again and again by a furious bull, the wretched animal uttering plaintive cries as he received fresh wounds before he lay down to die, and doing his poor best with teeth and legs to defend himself against his infuriated foe. This little episode was saluted with shouts of laughter from a thousand throats, while cries of *bravo, toro!* rent the air. I could bear it no longer, but getting up hastily from my seat, made the best of my way into the open air.

Apart from the disgusting nature of the spectacle, which was like the horrors of a slaughter-house or knacker's yard many times multiplied dished up for the amusement of a multitude, sanctioned by the chief authorities of the town, and made gay with music, banners, and bright colours; the excitement of the spectators, and their more than *indifference* to animal suffering, were the noticeable features of this most popular of Spain's *funciones*. The assembled thousands alternately cheered the bull or abused him; praised the *picadores* or *espada,* or loaded them with vituperation; and all this time *girls*, *children*, and *ladies* were looking on and applauding; and one pretty girl of eighteen, *du peuple*, it is true, was sucking oranges and eating buns during the horrid butchery to which I have alluded.

But enough of the oft-told tale. No Englishman will ever be persuaded to look upon it as fair sport, where the horse, poor wretched hack as he may be, is led *blindfold* to the slaughter, and is brought into the arena for no other purpose than to be mangled and torn; and no Spaniard probably will ever be convinced but that the game is a most noble one, which his countrymen and their descendants only are capable of conducting, and which, indeed, none but " *gentes de pelo en pecho*," as they vauntingly describe themselves, could carry to a successful issue.

LETTER XXII.

SARAGOSSA TO BARCELONA.

COMPANIONSHIP BY THE WAY—LERIDA—MANRESA—
MONTSERRAT—GRAND APPEARANCE—A SPLENDID
PROSPECT—ARRIVAL AT BARCELONA—BEAUTIFUL
SITUATION—BUSY ASPECT OF ITS STREETS AND SHOPS
—CATHEDRAL—VIEW OF THE CITY FROM MONTJUIS.

Fonda de las Cuatro Naciones, Barcelona;
April 2, 1872.

I ARRIVED here about ten last night, having had fourteen hours' travelling, and a delay of nearly an hour and a half at the station on arrival, *waiting for luggage*, a not unusual *cosa de España*.

I had met at the *table d'hôte* at Saragossa a Captain and Mrs. B—. The gentleman accompanied me to the bullfight, and as we were travelling the same road, we joined company and occupied the same compartment in the railway.

The first part of the journey exhibited the

like dreary characteristics to which I have so often alluded—the wild, uncultivated tracts of land, followed by grubbed-up fields and black vine stumps, interspersed with rock, mountain, and torrent. Portions of the land seemed to have been torn to pieces by heavy floods, and I should think the embankment of the railway must at times run serious risks during the storms to which in certain seasons the country is liable.

We dined at Lerida, a largish place, and discovered we had entered Catalonia by the change in the peasants' head-covering. In lieu of the handkerchief round the forehead we observed the Masaniello cap, which is not allowed, however, to hang on the shoulder, but the tail is caught up and tacked underneath the crown.

The interest of the road improved just before reaching Manresa, an important town, strongly situated on a precipitous height. It boasts some large cloth factories, and near it, I was informed by a Spanish fellow-traveller, were some coal mines. I saw for myself that both steam- and water-power were being used, and that there was more evidence of activity about the place than I had yet beheld.

It was on approaching Manresa that we came in sight of that most celebrated and extraordinary mountain, Montserrat. It rose into the clear evening sky, bare, grey, and jagged like a saw—hence its name—in the grandest manner, and as the rail turns and winds very much when in its vicinity, you have a constantly different view every quarter of an hour. From one point it was truly magnificent. At our feet was a torn ravine, through which a torrent was rushing, and whose jagged banks were covered with pines, while the eye was carried on from rock to mountain in almost endless succession till it reached the little village, above which the mountain rose, in infinite majesty and splendour. Decidedly the grandest view I have yet seen in Spain.

From this point, and before we reached it, we passed through several tunnels and deep cuttings, which must have made the construction of the line both difficult and costly, and then it fell dark. There was nothing now left to do, but shut our eyes and wait patiently for Barcelona, where, on arrival, as I have mentioned, the great virtue, patience, of which a traveller in Spain should be provided with a large stock, had to be still further exercised, till the lady grew faint and sick, and no wonder, for we had dined poorly on the road at twelve, and it was then nearly ten at night. However, everything comes to an end, and so did our tribulation, and this *really comfortable* hotel received us at last.

Barcelona reminds me a good deal of Bordeaux. There are the same fine square houses, some of them with marble staircases and entrance halls, the same appearance of bustle and business, a rare thing in Spain, and, therefore, the more remarkable when made manifest. But it has one signal advantage, to my mind, over Bordeaux, that is, of being placed upon the sea—the crisp, blue Mediterranean—which looks charming this morning as it glitters under the bright sun.

Vegetation is much more advanced here. The sycamores which adorn the *Rambla* or public walk running from the sea to the country and dividing the town in two, on which our hotel is situated, are out in leaf, and already begin to yield a welcome shade. The Barcelona shops are much finer and better supplied than those of Madrid, and I certainly should prefer it as a residence if I were compelled—as I hope I never shall be —to live in Spain.

There is a charming walk on the seaboard or rampart which, like that of Genoa, overlooks the port. As it stands at a right angle to the *Rambla* it makes, with the latter, a continuous promenade, and the evening being mild both have been filled with people enjoying the air. This *muralla del mar* must be a great boon in the hot summer nights, as there is always a pleasant freshness coming from the sea, and they only who have been compelled to breathe the stifling atmosphere of the streets in these southern, and not too well-drained, towns, in the hot season, can thoroughly appreciate the luxury of such a *paséo*.

Barcelona boasts some very ancient

churches. The *Seo* or Cathedral was commenced at the end of the thirteenth century upon the site of a pagan temple, and is dedicated to Sta. Eulalia, whose body is supposed to lie in a chapel below the high altar. The building is gothic, has two charming towers, and is full of curious sculptures both in wood and stone. The stalls of the choir are particularly beautiful, each of them being adorned with a gothic spire of most elaborate carving.

Santa Maria del Mar is another most interesting church, and the *Calle de la Plateria*, or Silversmiths' Street, leading to it, has much to attract and repay attention.

Barcelona seems well supplied with provisions of all kinds, and I saw more flowers exposed for sale than have hitherto met my eye.

Having thoroughly explored the town I strolled out into the country in the direction of the Montjuis, which rises majestically to the right of the city, looking seawards, and is crowned with some imposing fortifications. Climbing nearly to the summit, along a zig-zag road, edged with occasional aloes and prickly pears, I enjoyed a magnificent view, the town lying at my feet, and the coast line clearly defined, and the dark blue sea, flecked with patches of white sails, stretching out for many a league. Altogether the picture was a very fine one.

Rumours of political disturbances, consequent on the elections are flying about from mouth to mouth, and a gentleman at the *table d'hôte* seriously advised me not to think of visiting Tarragona as it was in a most uneasy state. Finding, however, upon close enquiry, that he could furnish me with no other ground for his warning than mere hearsay, I shall not allow it to stand in the way of prosecuting my journey.

LETTER XXIII.

BARCELONA TO TARRAGONA.

ENVIRONS OF BARCELONA—FINE MOUNTAIN SCENERY—LOFTY SITUATION OF TARRAGONA—PICTURESQUE HOUSES — CATHEDRAL — CLOISTERS — ROMAN AQUEDUCT—PARTY SPIRIT.

> Fonda de Paris, Tarragona;
> *April* 4, 1872.

IN company of Captain and Mrs. B— I left Barcelona in the afternoon of yesterday and arrived here at night.

It is not a change for the better. Barcelona is the most comfortable of all the Spanish towns I have yet visited. The hotel was excellent—clean, and well-managed. It was kept, as is the present one, by Italians, and I am informed that all the best hotels in the Peninsula are under similar management.

Tarragona is in strong contrast to the city

I have left. In place of a flourishing, well-built town, I find myself amid ruins, and in lieu of rows of bright shops filled with a variety of wares and little crowds collected round them, I wander through dark, crooked lanes, almost denuded of inhabitants.

But I have not spoken of the journey hither, yet it is worth recording, for I have so often had occasion to depict barrenness and desolation, that it is a pleasing duty to change the colours of my palette.

Let me, then, hasten to tell you that the environs of Barcelona as seen from the rail are charming. The valley you pass through before striking among the mountains offers the aspect of a garden in which everything seems to grow. There are many fine villas with grounds full of orange trees covered with fruit from whose balconies and terraces the most beautiful views can be enjoyed. The banks bristle with aloes as along the *riviera*, and altogether the aspect of the landscape is smiling and fruitful.

On approaching Martorell, the soil was of the richest red, like parts of Devonshire;

vines were growing abundantly and coming into leaf, and figs and olive-trees sprang up from every available spot of ground.

Lovers of mountain scenery would have found much to admire, for chain appeared above chain, distinguishable from each other by some splendid effects of light and shadow, and in the misty distance once again rose the hoary Montserrat which was so distinguishable a feature on our way from Lerida.

On nearing Tarragona the line ran close to the sea-shore, whereon the waves were lazily beating, whilst on the other side appeared some thick underwood, which clothed a rising ground, and offered admirable cover for smugglers and other marauders who, from time immemorial, have infested these thinly populated and almost inaccessible fastnesses.

The railway station abuts upon a busy and dirty little port, where an English traveller will notice with some amusement the announcement of *Calle* Smith at a street corner, and it seems quite another journey (when you undertake it for the first time) to reach the town of Tarragona proper. It is built upon a lofty rock, some eight hundred feet above the sea-level, was once surrounded by extensive and massive fortifications, but successive sieges have so battered them down that they present nothing at the present day but a picture of hopeless ruin,—grey, ugly and menacing.

The street in which my hotel is situated is straight and level, containing some decent houses, but on emerging from it in your ascent to the cathedral (for the sacred building is placed at the apex of the mount), you must clamber up unpaved lanes and alleys so crooked and narrow that no wheeled carriage could by possibility ascend them. This, however, is but of little moment in a country where every burthen is conveyed on the patient and convenient back of an ass or mule.

The houses are of great antiquity, but seem dirty and uncared for. As places of *residence* they are by no means desirable, but they are so strangely composed of bits and fragments of other buildings that almost every separate habitation is a study. Stones with Roman and Moorish inscriptions are let into walls; an open gateway discloses a broken pillar, once the support of a Pagan temple, into which a ring has been set to attach a mule to. The whole place is, in fact, crammed full of pictures. An artist would delight in it. You turn a corner and come upon some nondescript building, in which the Roman, the Goth, the Moor and the Christian have each had a part. It is surmounted, perhaps, by a broken terrace, over which at once wave the palm, the aloe, the prickly pear and the orange, showing how far south I have wandered; and then, the peeps of the blue Mediterranean, through some Gothic or Roman arch are simply delicious. Owing, naturally, to the elevated position of the city, many portions of it offer magnificent views, both of the sea and surrounding country, and there is plenty of food for reflection in the noble prospects thus opened before you, and the foreground of ruins and jumbling of ancient and modern materials that I have just alluded to.

I paid an early visit to the cathedral, which, as I before observed, is at the very summit of the rocky mount on which Tarragona is placed. After clambering up to the top of a crooked street, you reach the Market Place, whence a broad flight of steps conducts you to the sacred edifice.

The façade is in the shape of a triangle, with a splendid rose window, and there is a most interesting portal, in whose deeply recessed sides are gothic niches, containing effigies of the apostles. These works date back to the end of the thirteenth and the middle of the fourteenth centuries. The doorway is most singular, being divided by a figure of the Virgin and Child, with the Saviour, Popes, and Emperors praying in various attitudes above.

The interior is very striking, with a grand simplicity about it that is wonderfully attractive. The transept has some magnificently-painted windows, and there are some most curious bas-reliefs, representing the marvellous history of a *Santa Tecla*, who, like *Sta. Eulalia* of Barcelona and the *Madonna del*

Pilar of Zaragoza, worked more miracles than the sacred writings attribute to the Saviour himself.

Some of the chapels are richly ornamented, and there are many fine old tombs and antique carvings that will well repay careful examination. The cloisters in their comparative minuteness reminded me of the Campo Santo of Pisa. Like the latter there is a garden in the centre, whilst the walls and enclosure form a perfect museum of antiquity. The numerous invaders of the Peninsula have played sad havoc with the ornamental pointed windows, and a little world of memories is summoned to the mind on observing in unmistakable English characters the words " 6th Company " painted on the wall.

On my descent from the cathedral I met Captain B— and his wife in the little omnibus belonging to the hotel about to visit an interesting Roman aqueduct at a few miles distance on the road to Lerida, and at their invitation I joined company.

Having cleared all the ruts and huge stones

which lay in our path during the descent to the high road without serious accident, although not without considerable discomfort, we pursued the rest of our journey in tolerable ease, and after nearly an hour's drive, we came upon the object of our search.

Spanning a valley from hill to hill, and with a height in the centre of nearly a hundred feet, this aqueduct, known as the *Puente de Ferreras*, and built of a dusky red stone, looks both graceful and imposing. The arches stand in two tiers, there being eleven below and twenty-six above, and the entire length is stated at 700 feet. I walked along the top of it to about the middle to enjoy the view which, although not very extensive, has a singular charm from the contrasts of colour and the deep solitude of the valley.

Tarragona had a fine, not to say imposing, look as we approached it on our return. The mountainous scenery on the left, the dark sea on the right, and the city standing upon its rugged mount crowned by the old cathedral in the centre, formed a splendid prospect, made the more grand by menacing clouds which covered half the sky, and left mere patches of blue and white as if to render more impressive the huge billows of vapour that rolled slowly along.

My chance friends and I part company tomorrow morning. We are all going to Valencia, but they travel there direct whilst I start a day later in order that I may visit Reus. We shall doubtless meet again, for they will not quit Spain without seeing Andalusia.

I have looked in vain during my stay here for any signs of the disturbances with which I was threatened when at Barcelona, but, *en revanche*, I am warmly counselled not to go to Valencia for an identical reason. That party spirit runs high just now in Spain there can be little doubt, for not even the neutral ground of the *table d'hôte* has been sacred from the clamour of the politician. At Burgos and at Valladolid the discussions were noisy and prolonged, and so warm did the disputants wax at Pamplona that I should scarce have been surprised if they had come to blows.

In the general demeanour of the people out of doors, however, I perceive little of that excitement which is supposed to be so prevalent, and I shall refuse to believe in the existence of danger to the inoffensive traveller till I have substantial reason to alter my opinion.

LETTER XXIV.

REUS.

UNEASY PAVEMENT—GENERAL DULNESS—APPEARANCE OF THE COUNTRY.

Fonda de Paris, Tarragona;
April 5, 1872.

REUS is a second and very inferior edition of Tarragona. At least, the latter is on a hill and affords magnificent views; and it is also on the sea, which always has a charm. But Reus is inland, lies in a plain, and possesses, *comme surcroît de malheur*, all Tarragona's worst features. The streets are either totally unpaved or have but a few stones left here and there, which jut out like the teeth from the poor dismantled jaws of the very old. You may imagine what travelling over them is in a vehicle, and more especially in such a vehicle as a Reus omnibus. I thought I should have either every bone in my body dislocated as I went from the station in the omnibus, or that I should fracture my skull, for I was flying between the seat and the roof every few seconds like a skylark just caged.

I breakfasted there at the best *fonda* in the place, which was the old *parador* of the diligences. Having performed that office to the best of my ability, for the fare was of the toughest and rankest, and quietly listened to the excited talk of a group of citizens at the other end of the table, who seemed full of the elections that had resulted, as far as Reus was concerned, greatly in favour of the republican candidate, I had three hours within which to visit the town.

I soon discovered that, short as that time was, it was more than sufficient to familiarise me unpleasantly with a place where the streets are only crooked and doubtful lanes, and there is but one building, the cathedral, to *look at*, certainly not to admire.

To make matters worse it came on to rain and hail very heavily, and I was forced to take refuge under the arches of the only square which, like every other I have yet seen in Spain, has been recently baptized *Plaza de la Constitucion*. There I smoked my cigar till the rain held up, pestered by beggars (who had taken refuge there like myself), or stared at by the lounging lazzaroni-looking population.

At last the rain-clouds blew over, the sun broke through, and, tired of the town, I strolled a mile or two into the country. It is wonderfully fertile, being under capital irrigation, and the amount of olive trees and vines is very great. I passed a villa or two also boasting groves of palms and orchards of orange trees, the fine ripe fruit with which the latter were covered shining pleasantly in the now clear blue atmosphere.

I returned here in time for dinner, and having finished that important ceremony (quite alone to-day), I have come up to my room to finish these hasty lines.

To-morrow morning I leave for Valencia (twelve more hours), from which city I will write again.

I cannot say much in favour of the beauty

of the Catalonian women. At Zaragoza I *did* see some nice faces and fine figures, but I have looked for them in vain since I left that town.

LETTER XXV.

TARRAGONA TO VALENCIA.

RICHNESS OF VEGETATION — TEDIOUS TRAVELLING — ORANGE PLANTATIONS—THEIR WEALTH—CATHEDRAL —ABSENCE OF MONKS AND FRIARS.

Fonda Villa de Madrid,
Valencia; *April* 7, 1872.

QUITTING the picturesque but dilapidated old town of Tarragona at ten in the morning by the train coming from Barcelona, I arrived here late last night, half stupefied with headache, but with my brain full of the images of beauty that had been impressed upon it all through the journey.

Parts of the road, indeed, were very fine, and nothing can surpass the fertility of this favoured tract, where everything vegetable seems to flourish, and where a soil and sun exist which produce alike the fruits of Europe, Asia, and Africa.

The line runs along the sea-coast, sometimes close on to the shore, and for many miles you are hemmed in between the sea and the mountains. When drawing near any town, such as Tortosa, where in a delta you cross the mouths of the Ebro, or Castellon de la Plana, the gardens of the houses are filled with orange trees (fortunately not all gathered), figs, vines, pomegranates, and palms. Sometimes they are all inextricably mingled, and very charming did an occasional lonely building look—some remnant of the Moor—with a tall palm rising by its side majestically into the golden atmosphere of this southern region.

But you have to put up with a large amount of fatigue in order to get at such pictures, and I am sure that you, ever ready as you are to appreciate all that is lovely in art and nature, would not have the physical strength to bear up against it.

You must remember that you cannot break your journeys, and ten and twelve hours must often be calculated upon, with poor food and not very good accommodation when you are at the journey's end.

In the midst of plenty the people seem to live miserably, and having no idea of comfort and very little of cleanliness, they cannot comprehend or they despise the fastidiousness of foreigners. Smoking is so universal that no man ever thinks of inquiring whether his cigar or cigarette is unpleasant to his neighbour, male or female. But *very few* women travel, and to one woman at a table you will find twenty men. And they smoke between the courses; they smoke in the railway carriage; they smoke in all offices, public and private; they smoke right into the very doorways of their churches and theatres, and in all the rooms of all the houses. The omnibus which takes you to or from any station is filled with smokers, and driver and porters alike have cigarettes incessantly lolling from the corners of their mouths.

A landed proprietor and his wife got into the compartment of our carriage a few stations before arriving at Valencia. The lady had a basket of magnificent oranges, which she liberally presented all round, and she held in her hand the bough of an orange tree, upon which there were *twenty*, each as big as the fist. The gentleman pointed out to me his own plantation as the line passed it. There must have been a hundred trees in the portion I saw, and which, like an apple orchard in Kent, were laden with fruit, so that many of the boughs had to be propped up with stakes. Two crops are got off these trees during the year, and my informant told me that several of the trees would produce upwards of *a thousand*, and would be worth a pound sterling a tree per year!

I have been wandering great part of the day through the narrow and tortuous streets of the city. The town has no special attraction, but it contains some fine and even palatial buildings, more especially in the *Calle de Caballeros*, which, as its name implies, is an aristocratic quarter. There is, I learn, a good deal of an inferior kind of alabaster in the neighbourhood, of which several of the door-jambs and caryatides supporting the terraces, richly sculptured, are composed; and there are many houses decorated in the

Moresque style, with the beautiful horseshoe arch. The most noticeable of the Valencian palaces is the one alongside of my hotel, belonging to the family of the " *Dos Aguas.*" I say the most *noticeable*, but it is rather from its elaborate alabaster ornaments, which crowd the façade from "pediment to basement," than from its architectural beauty.

The cathedral is a strange jumble of styles, Gothic, Corinthian, and nondescript. It boasts some fine paintings by Juanes, Ribalta, and others, but, as usual, there reigns throughout the building such a semi-darkness that there is no chance of ascertaining whether the works be true or false, masterpieces of art or simply effective daubs.

Many of the men in this part of the Peninsula are dark as Africans, but I have been surprised to see the quantity of women having fair, that is to say, light brown hair, some even red. There has been evidently a great admixture of race, and I should not be at all surprised if many of the present generation owe their origin to French or English parentage, as the soldiers of both nations were for some time resident here during the frightful wars which have so torn and devastated the country. I still look in vain for *beauty*, and if I do not find it in Andalusia I shall leave Spain with many preconceived opinions altered, and quite "corrected" on that and indeed on many other points regarding this country.

The beggars are as numerous, as importunate, and as hideous as they were in Tuscany a quarter of a century ago. They literally swarm, and you cannot enter a church or gaze at a building without being at once surrounded, and having your sensibility shocked by the frightful deformities with which humanity is occasionally visited.

One thing has specially struck me by its *absence*. I have not seen a single *monk* or *friar* in Spain. True, many of the monasteries have been suppressed, but I expected at least to find as many of these gentry in the Peninsula as one meets with in Italy.

I leave here to-morrow at 3 p.m., and shall have to travel all night till nearly nine the following morning before I can reach Madrid. *There*, however, I hope to be indemnified by getting letters from all the dear friends I have left behind me.

LETTER XXVI.

VALENCIA.

EFFECTS OF IRRIGATION—TRAIN STOPPED BY BRIGANDS —THE ALAMEDA—SPLENDID "PLAZA DE TOROS."

Valencia;
April 7, 1872.

I WROTE to you from Barcelona, and have since travelled down the east coast of the Mediterranean to this city, once so dear to the Moors, stopping a couple of days at Tarragona by the way.

Nothing can exceed the fertility of the country along this coast line. With few exceptions, it is a continuous garden, where everything seems to grow. The system of irrigation created by the Moors is still kept up, and as the soil is wonderfully fecund you see at the same time all kinds of vegetable produce, orange trees heavy with golden fruit, vines bursting into leaf, forests of carob trees and gigantic olives, barley already in ear, rice and other cereals, and on the heights in sheltered spots the palm embracing the cypress.

The ranges of mountains are not less beautiful, and I counted no fewer than *six*, one behind the other, exhibiting every gradation of blue, according to their distance from the eye. As spurs of these mountains descend, in many instances, right down into the sea, and for miles are at no great distance from it, they were admirably adapted in the old times, ironically styled "the good," for the retreat of robbers by land and sea, and, indeed, it is not so many years agone since the very road I traversed was such that men carried their lives within their hands.

The noble profession of brigandage is far from being extinct, even now. You have read, doubtless, in the English papers, that no further back than last week the train from Cordova to Madrid was run off the line through the "precaution" of a band of armed men tearing up some of the metals, which brought the whole convoy to a stand. It is perfectly true. The train was rifled of what treasure it was conveying, and although none of the passengers were robbed, a young comedian by the name of Ibañez, through not obeying quickly enough the order to lie down *face à terre*, was so ill-treated that he has since died.

Report attributes this atrocious act to a Carlist band, and the non-robbery of the passengers gives some colour to the rumour. But you may conceive from the fact of such an outrage that travelling in Spain, even at this present writing, is not unmixed with that dash of danger and adventure which removes it from the ordinary smoothness of railway voyaging elsewhere.

For my own part I have little doubt but that the roads will be safer now for some weeks to come. At least I hope so, for as I am going to traverse a portion of the road referred to to-morrow night, and have not the slightest wish to have my head damaged by a Spanish *ladron* or political *exalté*, I would rather reach my destination at the proper time and with a whole skin.

The city of Valencia retains much of its old Moorish character, as visible in the decoration of many of the houses and the narrow tortuous streets. The environs are extraordinarily fruitful; and a public garden, the Alameda, I have just visited on the other side of the Turia torrent (which, by-the-bye, is crossed by two fine bridges) has tens of thousands of roses all blooming at once, orange trees laden with fruit and flowers, stocks and ranunculuses in the richest variety of colour, hyacinths, guelder roses, oleanders, and a host of other plants, all blossoming together.

The *Plaza de Toros*, close to the railway station, is the finest I have yet seen, and is, I am informed, the grandest in Spain. It is built of brick in the style of a Roman amphitheatre, that is to say, with tier above tier of arches towards the street instead of the usual plain, blank, plaster building, looking like the shambles, which the plaza really becomes.

The weather is exceedingly pleasant just now, and some occasional showers of rain only add to the beauty, for the sun afterwards bursts through with a splendour natural to this favoured clime.

LETTER XXVII.

VALENCIA TO MADRID.

FESTIVAL OF SAN VICENTE, THE PATRON OF VALENCIA—VIEW FROM SUMMIT OF SAN MIGUEL—ORANGE PLANTATIONS—WONDERFUL FERTILITY—ALCINA—FEAST OF ROSES—LA ENCINA—ARANJUEZ—FINE VIEW OF MADRID.

Madrid;
April 9, 1872.

IF you get a confused letter to-day, pray attribute it to the right cause—my having been travelling for nineteen consecutive hours. The night was fortunately mild and beautiful, succeeding a day as like a lovely one in June in England as possible.

When I quitted Valencia it was in high festival—the baptismal day of San Vicente, the patron of the city, and as he had distinguished himself in his lifetime by burning no end of heretics as a Grand Inquisitor, and kicking the devil out of his cell when His Satanic Majesty presented himself in the guise of a beautiful woman, he is thus properly honoured, for his Christian piety and rare continence, after his death. It is a strange thing to see the business of a whole busy town stopped, and all manner of junketings going on, because a sanguinary fanatic "played such pranks" as must "have made the angels weep," between 400 and 500 years ago.

Little theatres were erected in most of the street corners and *plazas*, where his "miracles" were being enacted in the open air by young boys "dressed in the costume of the period," before a gaping multitude varying in numbers from some scores to some hundreds according to the attraction of the *funcion*. I must say that the audiences or spectators were not particularly reverent, but smoked and chatted and spat and laughed as they would have done if it had been a "Punch and Judy show," to which, indeed, it bore no very remote resemblance as Master Vicente,

like Master Punch, was very ready with the
" lethal weapon."

I also mounted to the top of the campanile of the cathedral, San Miguel, whence I enjoyed a most magnificent view. The city, almost circular, lay like a map at my feet. The open courts of the houses were exposed to my inspection as if I had been another Asmodeus, and very curious did the town appear with its thronged and crooked streets, its waving banners and groups collected round the little theatres to which I have alluded. The *vega* or plain beyond the city walls presented to the eye the greatest varieties of green, and I would recommend every traveller who wishes to form an idea of the teeming fertility of the Valencian district to clamber up this ancient tower.

The road from Valencia due southwards to La Encina, where I dined and it fell dark, runs through a paradise of verdure, where the fruits of every climate seem to flourish. The orange, the palm, the olive, the vine, the carob were equally rich and productive; the barley was in ear, the corn nearly three feet high. Rice and the mulberry for the silk-worm succeeded plots of vegetable produce; the earth was sparkling with every tinge of green, and overhead was a canopy of lapis-lazuli blue. Never have I seen such vegetation before, and perhaps no spot on earth can exceed it in fertility.

But the orange plantations! say rather the orange thickets—orange *forests*—for as far as the eye could reach the trees stood in their rich sheeny green rows, and where the fruit had been plucked the portion turned towards the south was white with blossom, from which the scent, as the gentle wind blew over it, was " full to overflowing." So lovely was the sight that, alone in the compartment of the carriage, I found myself involuntarily clasping my hands with wonder, tears filled my eyes, and my heart leaped with joy and veneration towards the Creator of such overpowering beauty.

Many points of the road before reaching the junction at La Encina are worthy of special remark. At Alcina many really pretty girls came on to the platform, and it being a *fiesta* were very smartly dressed. Each had a bouquet of roses in her hand, and, indeed, a rose was in everybody's hand —evidently a "feast of roses." Jativa with its castle, and houses grouped at the foot of bold crags, was singularly picturesque; in fact, one saw pictures everywhere; roses were growing as in June with us; the hedges of some of the gardens were composed of them, and on approaching La Encina the train runs through a magnificent valley with finely contoured mountains on both sides.

As soon as daylight enabled me to see out of the carriage window, I remarked that all the rare beauty of landscape on which I had closed my eyes was gone. Again I found myself amongst treeless, unproductive land, bare hills with flat tops, yielding nothing but stones. The one green spot in the desert was Aranjuez, which is most richly wooded. I soon perceived the cause in delicious, clear-running rivulets, which carried fertility wherever they flowed.

The view of Madrid caught at a distance

of some three or four miles was very striking, extending, as it does, in a line on the ridge of many tawny hills, and grandly backed by the rocky Guadarrama, at that time covered with snow.

LETTER XXVIII.

MADRID.

GENERAL REMARKS ON TRAVELLING THROUGH SPAIN—
COUNTRY SINGULARLY UNINTERESTING—CAUSES OF
STERILITY.

Madrid;
April, 10, 1872.

A PAUSE in my rambles enables me to write you a few lines by way of assuring you that you dwell warmly in my remembrance, if such assurance be necessary, and of giving you some hasty impressions of the various scenes through which I have been carried. Indeed, this traversing a country by rail is not dissimilar to the unwinding of the canvas of the old panoramas, with the additional advantage of atmosphere and the bustling and novel spectacle presented by every petty station at which the train stops. And those same stations are very nearly endless. They occur at intervals of two or three leagues, and as the trains, postal or not, pull up at every one of them, the result is an average speed of *ten miles an hour*. The iron horse does not, therefore, in this part of the world hurry you along at a rate which prevents the eye dwelling upon any particular object. The lines not unfrequently follow the old road, for the simple reason that a country so mountainous as this has left but little choice for either but to follow the valley or natural pass; and when those same mountains had to be crossed, the engineers of the lines were able to select no better track than that originally chosen by the ordinary roadmakers.

Down to this present writing I have traversed the kingdoms of New and Old Castille, Leon, Aragon, Navarre, Catalonia, and Valencia. I am on the eve of starting southwards for my final journey before quitting Spain for England, and shall cross Don Quixote's country and the far-famed Andalusia from end to end. I have visited the cities of Burgos, Valladolid, Madrid, Saragossa, Pamplona, Barcelona, Tarragona, and

Valencia, from which last town I came back yesterday, having travelled the greater part of a day and one night.

A man who comes into Spain and makes his way simply to Madrid, although it stands in the very centre of the Peninsula would have but the faintest and the most erroneous notion of what the kingdom really contains. In fact, nothing can be more dreary than the whole journey after passing the Pyrenees to the capital. The passage of the mountain barrier at Irun and Hendaya has nothing in common with the grandeur of the Alpine passes from Switzerland or Savoy into Italy. If interested in engineering works he will, of course, admire the fine viaducts and tunnels over and through which the road is carried; but those passed, he will, after traversing some pastoral scenes in the north-east corner of Spain, come upon a desolate, howling wilderness, without a tree, scarcely a shrub; a vast table-land, up which (for the road rises constantly to Madrid till it reaches at the capital a height of 2400 above the sea level) the train labours; and the only change the traveller sees from the endless duns and browns of the landscape is a territory of rocks and stones, varying in size from a big house to a pebble, and of every shape that nature has been tempted to mould.

The improvident and ignorant people have felled every tree, owing to the fancy of its interfering with the growth and ripening of the crops. As a natural consequence, there being *no shade* and no powerful roots beneath the soil to help to bind it together, the intense suns of the Spanish summers have dried the ground through and through, and the rains of winter have made torrents overflow, and have washed the loosened earth into the lower lands, or swept it away in solution to the sea; so that vast tracts, which in former times might have been productive, are sterile for evermore, because the rising grounds have been reduced to a *skeleton*. The people try to make up by artificial irrigation for their own idiocy in interfering with a beneficent Nature; but bleed the torrents as they will, and as they do, until the river beds get occasionally as dry as the high road, the source of supply is far too scanty for their wants, and droughts will not unfrequently occur which kill the cattle by thousands and reduce the unfortunate agriculturists to the last extremities of suffering.

This hasty sketch will explain the want of interest that is to be derived from the aspect of the landscape in nearly one half of Spain. A journey, then, into Valencia—where the perfection of irrigation was introduced by the Moors (which is still kept up), and where one of the most delicious climates under Heaven is to be enjoyed—is like a glimpse of Paradise. The vegetable products of Europe and Africa here meet on a ground which is equally favorable to both; the earth is full of the richest verdure, and for background you have a range of noble mountains, chain beyond chain, till the last melts into the colour of the sky.

The interest to be found in the other parts of Spain to which I have alluded, where the country presents the aspect of utter desolation, lies, of course, in its ancient cities, where traces are in some to be discovered of the Roman and the Goth, in others of the Moor;

but where, unfortunately, still more ineffaceable marks remain of the destructive *Christian* in former and more recent wars. The cathedrals of Burgos, Valladolid, and Saragossa—those of Barcelona and Tarragona are charming—many of the old palaces, have an attraction in their decay which you will thoroughly understand; the costumes of the people, more especially of the lower class, are curious and worthy of study; but you have to put up, for all this sight-seeing, with poor lodging, dirt, discomfort, wretched food, filthy and importunate beggars, and a host of "petites misères" too numerous to mention, but easy to conceive.

LETTER XXIX.

MADRID.

A CHARMING PICTURE—A VILLA IN THE PRADO—DISLIKE OF THE SPANIARDS TO THE COUNTRY—AN ENGLISH DINNER—RUDENESS OF THE MADRILEÑOS TOWARDS THE KING—INNER LIFE OF THE SPANIARDS.

Madrid;
April 11, 1872.

I AM on the eve of my departure for Andalusia, so that you may expect my next to be dated from Cordova, where I am due to-morrow at one, having to travel all night and half the day.

After my last letter was posted I called upon my friend Mr. B—, who had hitherto been absent from Madrid, and accepted an invitation to dine with him yesterday. As he lives at the extremity of the Prado in a new detached villa (a few of which have sprung up in that locality, by far the most agreeable in the capital), we strolled towards it in the afternoon through the public walk, which, as usual, was crowded with pleasure seekers on foot and in carriages.

On one of the seats placed like those in Hyde Park along the main walk, we found a fine specimen of an Englishman, Captain W——, of the British Navy, to whom I was introduced by Mr. B——. Having whiled away half an hour in observing the moving throng, Captain W——, learning that I was fond of pictures, induced me to visit his house hard by, that I might inspect one of which he was evidently proud.

And well he might be, for rarely have I seen a painting of such mingled originality, quaintness and beauty. It represented a Magdalene, life-size, and more than half draped, lying on a bank, her head supported by one hand, the crucifix in the other, while groups of Cupids were hovering about her, covering her with roses. In the left hand corner appeared the following verse, apparently from Solomon's Song:

"Fulciteme floribus, stipateme mælis, quia amore langueo," &c; -

the English version running :

"Stay me with flowers, comfort me with apples, for I am sick of love."

Of the painter nothing was known. Its owner inclined to the belief that the work was Italian. That it was original there could be but little doubt, for not only was the execution of a very superior order, but the mode of treatment was too remarkable, for none of the many men who had seen it, travellers and artists, to remember a Magdalene with such an *entourage*, if its like had existed before. I gave it as my opinion that it was by a Spanish artist, or, if Italian, that it must have been painted in Spain at a time when the influence of the Inquisition was all-powerful. Nothing but the strict and sternly-enforced rules of the ultra-moral bigots of the period, in all things connected with outward show, would have induced an *Italian* artist, who delighted in representations of Nature "unadorned," to supply his Magdalene with such abundant clothing, and even to furnish his Cupids with other covering than their wings. Those Cupids were otherwise most deliciously painted, and might have been own brothers to some of the charming little "putti" of Albano. Captain W— had one or two other treasures in his little collection, but the "Magdalene," with her placid, soothing beauty, had a fascination which allowed you little attention for other objects.

Shortly after I reached Mr. B—'s villa, what was my astonishment on looking out of the drawing-room window, which opened on to the *paseo*, to find the drive and walks cleared as if by an enchanter's wand. On entering the gates leading into the garden, the carriages were four deep; the footpaths were thronged, and in a quarter of an hour there was not a living soul visible.

"That is the habit of the Spaniards," observed Mrs. B—, "they come together and they return together, like a flock of sheep or birds. They think us stark, staring mad for living out here. 'How can you exist,' they say, 'without cafés, without theatres, or a soul to talk to.' No Spaniard will, *alone*, dare to visit us after dark, although the whole promenade is lighted with gas from end to end. They say that there would be risk of assassination."

I could not help smiling and making the inquiry, who was left to assassinate since nobody would ever venture thither?

"Precisely so," she answered, "and more than that, it is my firm belief that the would-be assassin, if any such exist out of the imagination of a Spaniard, would be just as frightened to come along here after sundown as his intended victim."

We then went to dinner, which was an unusual treat, being thoroughly English in style; and an excellent leg of lamb was in evidence to prove what the country might produce if only the necessary intelligence were used in the breeding. I need not say that the joint in question was taken from an animal bred under Mr. B—'s directions.

Those only, who, like myself, had been fed for the last few weeks on stringy and tasteless meats, all disguised in the same doubtful sauce and on vegetables mixed with grease and garlic, could thoroughly appreciate the simple, well-cooked and nourishing meat, and the fine asparagus with white sauce which were put before me. And my enjoyment was made complete in the substitution of a bottle of excellent Bordeaux for the heavy, dark and flat-flavoured beverage, which I had hitherto imbibed under the *name* of Valdepeñas.

I took leave of my kind and courteous hosts at ten, smoking a cigar and looking at the stars, which, in this country, are inexpressibly large and beautiful, and I did not meet a single soul till within a few yards of the entrance to the Calle de Alcalá. On the seats there, at the *verge* of the walk, but in *sight* of the bustle of the streets were a few couples who had ventured *thus far* into the dreaded groves for the purpose of a little private converse and flirtation.

I omitted to mention that the King and Queen were in the drive in the afternoon in an open carriage, perfectly unattended; and with the ingrained loyalty proper to the

English character, we drew up to the rail as they passed and took off our hats, for which we were honoured by a most distinct recognition. The want of courtesy of the Spaniards towards Amadeo, simply because he is a foreigner, is as indecent as it is ill-bred. The footmen, seated behind their masters' carriages, keep their arms folded and stare at the young monarch as they drive past. Captain W— was very strong on the subject and hinted at a desire to horsewhip such offenders and their masters into the bargain to teach them better manners.

I learnt some curious particulars respecting these same carriage-folks from my two companions who had been some years resident in Madrid and knew the people well. Two thirds of all that grand outward show, they assured me, were a sham. The occupants of many of these handsome vehicles were miserably poor, and who, therefore, act in face of the world a continual masquerade. They live in wretchedness and dirt, and go all but in rags within doors that they may make a figure and put on a silk dress and a black coat *à la promenade*. Such things as dinner parties or parties of any kind among the Madrileños are unknown, for the simple reason that they are not only destitute of money but even of the decent paraphernalia of a dinner table, and it is only on rare occasions that one can get a sight of a Spanish interior. They will accept any treat the foreigner will offer them without a moment's hesitation, but never is it returned, so that the inhabitants of Madrid, the showy capital which seems so abounding in wealth, are, perhaps, more unsociable and inhospitable than the people of any other capital in Europe. They see their friends in the streets, or at church, but the interiors of their houses are mysteries to all but themselves.

How different a mode of life to that which is practised with us, where the inner comfort and the cleanliness and completeness of every part of the household are looked upon as essentials, in which an Englishman, and more especially an English*woman*, whose province it is, takes the greatest pride.

LETTER XXX.

MADRID TO CORDOVA.

DON QUIXOTE'S COUNTRY—WILDNESS OF THE ROAD—
RICH COLOURS OF THE FLOWERS—LINARES—MEN-
JIBAR — CORDOVA — ITS NARROW STREETS AND
MOORISH BUILDINGS—CHARMING *PATIOS*—COURT OF
ORANGES—THE MESQUITA—ANDALUSIAN WOMEN.

Cordova;
April 12, 1872.

ALTHOUGH I feel somewhat fagged this evening on account of having travelled all last night in a compartment so full as to be unable to stretch my legs, I cannot refrain from writing to you, for as I intend to leave for Seville to-morrow afternoon I may not have another early opportunity of doing so.

I left Madrid at nine last night, and was so miserably cramped in my corner and had such a hard seat, that with the first glimpse of daylight (about half past four), I directed my attention to the moving panorama visible from the window as the train crept slowly on.

There was nothing specially noticeable in the road, till a view was obtained of the Sierra Morena capped with snow. From that point the landscape improved, and there were a few very picturesque bits as we passed through the territory that Don Quixote has made famous, and observed the mills at which that gallant knight tilted. Doré has admirably hit off the characteristics of the country and people, and I shall be pleased on my return to again look over his excellent illustrations to Cervantes' inimitable story.

We passed the spot between Manzanares and Valdepeñas where a Carlist band only a few days previously made a train "stand and deliver." As I anticipated, the event had superinduced extra precautions. Not only had we a double allowance of civic guards in the train, but many were stationed along the line, and every petty station had its two or three.

The road was singularly wild and solitary

—just the place one would have selected for an exploit of the nature referred to—and as I looked round on my sleeping fellow-travellers and turned over in my mind the little chance there was of any of them offering any assistance in case of an attack, I noted our gradual drawing away from the inhospitable locality with unfeigned satisfaction.

Just before reaching Baeza there were some bits that the artist just referred to must surely have sketched and reproduced in his illustrations. A torrent tore its way through pointed crags,—grey, yellow and red—deliciously intermingled with trees, and the effect was rendered the more striking from the sun's rays darting through the mist generated at night in the *vega* and which was grandly rolling up the mountain side.

I must not omit to mention the wonderful vividness of the wayside flowers; the convolvulus, the poppy and the blue-bell displayed colours that were literally dazzling to the eye. The reappearance of the aloe, the prickly pear, and an occasional palm showed that we had got again into the region of the south, and out of that sterile zone in which Madrid is situated.

We passed Linares the station before Baeza, where the pigs of lead in the railway trucks hinted at the presence of the mines in the neighbourhood: later on, we arrived at Menjibar, where we breakfasted, and enjoyed quite a lively scene owing to the numerous arrivals by diligence from Granada and the Alhambra, who swelled our own numbers by the train.

At length, shortly after midday, Cordova itself came in sight. In 1845 Ford wrote of it:—" Cordova seen from the distance amid its olives and palm trees, and backed by the convent-crowned sierra has a truly oriental look; inside all is decay." If by decay he meant the want of life in the streets, it is precisely the same in 1872 as it was in 1845; but where in the name of wonder could any life appear in these narrow passages and lanes which run for a few yards, and then twist round a corner to end, nowhere in particular, except against a blank wall!

If you turn to a map of Cairo you will have

a notion—a little exaggerated, perhaps, but still a notion—of the disposition of the Cordovan streets. There is not one of them straight, and only two or three can boast of being wider than Pope's Head Alley or Finch Lane; and they are so thinly peopled that I traversed many without meeting a soul, although I became conscious that black eyes were watching me from the enclosed balconies above, which like a hareem window, are barred with iron and closely curtained.

There are but few of these same balconies towards the street; the one-story houses present, for the most part, the appearance of a dead wall, as there are no lower windows whatever; and altogether, the place had so deserted an air that I was inclined to fancy some mischievous elf had transported me to Pompeii, had twisted the straight streets of that town into distorted lines, had whitewashed the houses, and galvanized a few of its inhabitants into life, so strongly did this old Cordova remind me of the resuscitated Roman city.

Similar also to Pompeii the real *front* of the house is, to use a Hibernianism, at the *back* or rather in the *middle*; and as, instead of a street door, constantly closed, there is just within the doorway a wrought-iron gate, often of delicious workmanship, you are enabled to discern a pretty *patio* or court, open to the sky, surrounded by pillars which support the upper rooms, whilst the court itself is filled with flowers, (at this season, roses in every variety of species,) and orange trees whose blossom is as delicious to the scent as the fruit is to the eye. A fountain plays in the centre; the court is paved either with marble or encaustic tiles, the *azulejos* imitated from the Moors, and when the sun is too powerful, a striped awning is drawn over the open space above, and thus forms a temporary roofing.

The luxury of these open-air *patios* in a warm climate must be very great. The court being square and the breadth between the pillars and the wall sufficient, one side is always in shade, and at night the piano is wheeled out, or the guitar is produced, and nimble fingers soon set equally nimble feet a-capering.

The grand attraction, however, of Cordova is the cathedral, still called the *mezquita* from its having been the mosque of the Christian's predecessors. This monstrous building is indeed a wonder, the effect of which, on entering, takes your breath away. You are prepared for something peculiar and mysterious by the aspect of the Court of Oranges which you will first traverse. This court large as some London "squares," is surrounded by pillars with Moorish arches, its *Christian* addition being a marble pulpit at one extremity, whence San Vicente, (our old Valencian friend) urged upon his not unwilling hearers the advisability of burning some few thousand heretics, in order to ensure the safety of *their own souls*. The orange trees in this court are of vast size, many of the trunks being thicker than a man's body, and when I saw them they were studded as thickly with fruit as apple trees in a Kentish orchard.

Having taken in these natural beauties

and dwelt in memory on the horrors perpetrated here by man, enter the rather low-roofed building beneath the horse-shoe arch, and find yourself transported to the East, standing at the edge of a forest of marble! I say *a forest*, for that is exactly the effect of these thousand pillars, (the exact number is I believe 900), which spring from the marble pavement and support the roof.

I cannot describe to you the effect of perspective of these beautiful columns, scarcely two of them alike, but all of marble or granite. The moving figures seen in the half light at the extremity of one or other of these wonderful groves (nineteen in all) have a weird and striking appearance; and where some bit of stained glass admits a ray of sun, it irradiates that favoured space, and makes the contiguous vista the gloomier and more mysterious in consequence.

The comparatively modern Catholic *coro*, with its usual stall for the church dignitaries, and the chapels erected about the building, strike you as such wonderful anomalies, that like the proverbial fly in amber, when you come suddenly upon them, you wonder how the d—l they got there.

I cannot say much as yet of the Andalusian women. Those I have seen hitherto, had no pretensions to beauty or grace, though the eyes were fine. But they display a bit of coquetry which I have not observed elsewhere. Every girl, no matter her condition, directly her hair is dressed, sticks a natural flower in it, at this season a rose, a red one, which contrasts the best with her ebon hair. It seems strange to remark these common lasses, engaged in the coarsest occupations, with their heads adorned as if for the theatre, and perhaps without a stocking to their feet. I am informed that I shall find the custom universal throughout Andalusia. It is certainly pretty, and where there is a face to match, it must be very attractive.

A walk round the remains of the old wall of the City would furnish an artist with many capital little pictures. The squat, square tower shaded by an occasional palm tree, surrounded by that deliciously clear atmosphere, and more particularly as the sun is setting, when the whole heavens are aglow with vermillion, are as purely Oriental as anything he would find in the East.

And if that same artist's legs and lungs are in good order, let him mount, as I did, to the summit of the belfrey-tower, whence he will enjoy a rarely beautiful view. His commanding height will enable him to get a peep at the open *patios* of the houses and mark how numerous they are; he will derive amusement in tracing the tortuous streets, which seem to have been planned on the principle of a gigantic labyrinth; he will note the lazy course of the Guadalquiver towards Seville and the sea, made evident, where not actually visible, by the rows of trees; and he will be struck generally by the contrast of the whitewashed city with the green-pasture land which forms around it so pretty and appropriate a setting.

LETTER XXXI.

SEVLLLE.

ROAD FROM CORDOVA TO SEVILLE—ORANGES AND ALOES—
MOSQUITOES—ANDALUSIAN AND GIPSEY DANCES—
CATHEDRAL—THE GIRALDA—POMPEIAN ARRANGE-
MENTS.

Seville;
April 14, 1872.

ANOTHER stage upon my journey performed in comfort and safety, and by the time this letter reaches your hands, I trust to have arrived at my ultimate desination and to be, in fact, wending my way homewards.

It was a very pleasant trip from Cordova to this city, where I arrived about six o'clock after four hours run. The country here in the south, at least at this season of the year, is in wonderful contrast to the north and centre of Spain. The line runs through beautiful pasture ground, and as a consequence we have butter, and very good butter, once again. The vegetation is almost as rich as in Valencia though the land is not so highly cultivated. The oranges are very abundant, and at one little station, Palma del Rio, they lay in tens of thousands on the platform waiting for transport. The aloes are something marvellous; they seem to grow and most probably do grow spontaneously, and are used as hedgerows to divide the little fields from each other, and to mark the boundary of the line. A few of them were in flower, the stems rising to a height of some ten or fifteen feet, tapered at the top like a pine, and looking rarely beautiful with their multitudinous blossoms. It is no wonder if the process of flowering should kill the plant as the flower is out of all proportion to the parent stock. As the blossoms wither, the plant as if in sympathy, curls up and fades away till the huge stem stands bare and melancholy, the withered blossoms rustling in the breeze.

The little villages and towns visible from the carriage windows were unmistakably

Moorish; the houses of one story, whitewashed and with flat roofs for the enjoyment of the evening air. At every station the hedges of the little gardens were composed of delicious roses, red, white, and yellow, and which, like all the flowers in this part of the world, were of the most lively colours. The most beautiful were the blush-roses that looked in their delicate tints, exactly like those porcelain ones we have often admired in the windows of Paris, so perfect were they in shape, and so solid seemed their leaves and petals. Every girl who took her place in the train, and all her female companions who came to see her off, wore them in their hair, and some had huge bunches of these delicious flowers in their hands.

The line runs almost all the way by the side of the Guadalquiver, which in places is finely wooded, and at Carmona the river is crossed by an iron bridge. Like most of the continental streams which derive their origin from the mountain and flow uniformly towards the sea, the water is creamy yellow and turbid, carrying along in solution an immense quantity of the sandy soil through which it runs.

Lovely, however, as this country undoubtedly is, it has the serious drawback of being infested with mosquitoes, which commence their active operations in mid-spring and go on industriously all through the summer, dying off in the autumn or, as I should say, judging from past painful experience, migrating to Naples. The consequence of this visitation was, that I got a bad night, for although a good sleeper, I cannot rest where these pests abound. The warning blast of the well-known horn effectually banishes sleep from my eyelids, and I roused up a dozen times in the night to wage war with these tiny but *not insignificant* foes. I managed to slaughter one or two on each of these occasions, and when daylight began to revisit the earth, succeeded in getting an hour or two's slumber.

I came on here with a Mr. and Mrs. P— and a relative, Miss T—, besides two other ladies who had met them on the road. Congeniality of tastes made us at once sociable, and as we were all travelling in the same direction we resolved, as long as it was agreeable to each other, to keep together.

Hearing that an entertainment had been got up, for the benefit of such gentlemen in the hotel as chose to go, which should enable them to see some of the Andalusian and gipsey dances, Mr. P— and I gladly availed ourselves of the chance, and set off accompanied by the courier of that gentleman and the interpreter of the hotel who, to judge from his strong recommendation of the affair, had some interest in the result.

After traversing several streets, somewhat broader and less crooked, it is true, than those of Cordova, but still none of the widest and straightest, we reached a rough kind of assembly room, which we found to be occupied by about thirty gentlemen from the various hotels, and a sprinkling of the townspeople.

The performers were four girls (two of them decidedly pretty,) dressed in Andalusian costume with wonderfully rich satin skirts reaching to the knee, bare necks and arms, silk hose and white satin shoes. It was for all the world like being present at a *prova* of an opera, we, the spectators, being accommodated with chairs upon the stage. Some of their dances were very engaging, the castanets, with which they were all provided, keeping time, and making a natural accompanient to a mandolin and fiddle. The most characteristic performance was that executed by one of the girls, in walking costume with mantilla and fan, who was accosted, in dumb show, by a young fellow wrapped in the inevitable cloak. The various gradations of flirtation from the first glance through the different stages of acquaintanceship, in which the fan played a most conspicuous part—being now flirted, now closed with a sharp snap, now used as a shield, through the bars of which bright eyes glanced at the more and more ardent lover—were charmingly done; and his pursuit seemed to be crowned with success when, uncovering his cloak in the manner of Sir Walter Raleigh, he spread it on the ground and she stepped lightly over it. From that moment he was an accepted lover and they danced together to celebrate the event.

It was now the turn of the gipsies, of whom a dozen or so, men, women, and boys were present. Two women, with bare arms, their jetty hair nattily dressed and adorned with red roses, but with garments reaching to the ground, stood up in the centre of the room and, to the twanging of a guitar played by a burly fellow about forty, and the accompaniment of the voices of all their swarthy companions, in a lugubrious and discordant chant, began a strange series of posturing, moving in short circles back to back about each other, throwing out the hips and bringing their well-shod feet heavily to the ground after the manner of the niggers. In lieu of castanets they occasionally clapped their hands, an action that was imitated by all the gipsies together, who urged on the performers with loud " whoops " like those of a wild Indian, while the musician continued in a louder and louder key, his monotonous and unintelligible song. I was told that the words employed were not of the most decent character and if I could draw any meaning from the singular actions and postures of the dancers, I should incline to believe that my informant spoke truly. I call them dancers but, really, they but little deserved that name according to our notions of the steps that a dancer should execute. The performance struck me much more in the light of an antique religious ceremony, and there could be little doubt that it was derived from their Egyptian forefathers and was a remnant of some of the peculiar rites of that singular people. They continued till they were exhausted, when they were succeeded by another couple. There was, however, no change in the performance. Those who followed went through precisely the same antics and were more loudly applauded as their postures assumed a more indecent character. The whole thing was worth seeing, on account of its nationality and its diversity to any entertainment I had ever beheld before, and the dances of the Andalusians were really graceful and pleasing.

From the glimpse I obtained of Seville

last night I observed that it had many of the characteristics of Cordova, the houses having the same delicious *patios* or open-air courts, (filled with flowers and fountains in the centre) for the enjoyment of the bright or star-lit sky without going beyond the limits of the dwelling; and from my subsequent explorations by daylight I find it to be a large and handsome city, possessing some moderately broad and well-paved streets, with fewer of those tortuous lanes, strewn with "petrified potatoes," which do duty as a pavement in the ancient city alluded to. In the calle *de las Sierpes* there are some handsome shops and two of the finest cafés I have seen in Spain, paved with marble and richly decorated.

The city is filled with magnificent monuments, and many days might be profitably and delightfully spent in their examination. The cathedral, properly described as "the largest and finest in the Peninsula" is truly grand, and fills the mind with astonishment, both at the structure itself and the rich treasures of art which it contains. Sculpture and painting are represented by some wonderfully rich specimens; and the painted windows, of which the number is considerable, impart fine effects to this noble temple, although there is no doubt that they are destructive to oil paintings, and I have always held the opinion, which this visit to Seville cathedral has tended still further to confirm, that paintings in oil should be excluded from edifices where the light is admitted through stained glass.

The centre is as usual blocked up with the *coro*, but the two side aisles are clear and enable you to take in the stupendous dimensions of the building. Its proportions altogether are most harmonious and I attribute to this fact the strange delight one feels in wandering about it, pacing up one aisle and down another, without fixing the attention on any of the special details. And yet they are well worth careful study. Some of the tombs are remarkably fine; the high altar and its Gothic *retablo* are exquisite; the wood carving is, as usual perfect, and there is some very fine plate-work.

The pictures, some of them said to be by Murillo, were in too bad a light to enable me to see them properly, and others were tinged all the colours of the rainbow from the sun's rays either falling directly upon them through the stained glass, or from the colours being reflected from the marble pavement.

In such a fane, however, you seem to care little for accessories *per se*. Each in its place helps to swell the general effect, and that effect is, as I have before observed, simply superb.

On emerging from the cathedral I proceeded to the " Giralda," which like so many of the Italian " Campanili," is separate from the temple to which it belongs. It derives its name from the bronze figure at the summit used as a vane, which is so admirably posed that though of enormous size and weight it veers (*gira*) with the slightest breath of wind. Although now serving as the belfrey to the cathedral, great part of the tower, as its exquisite workmanship shows, owes its origin to the Moors, and dates back to the twelfth century; the upper portion being added as long after as the sixteenth. Unlike additions generally, the new portion is so admirably harmonised with the older structure that it would puzzle a far more critical eye than mine to detect the difference between the two. As it stands, this beautiful monument is in height about the same as that of St. Mark's at Venice, and you ascend it in the same way; that is, by inclined planes in the thickness of the wall in lieu of stairs.

You would be amused at my room at the hotel where I am now writing. It is a crib, like a Pompeian chamber, opening on to a marble-paved inner court, with arches supported by marble pillars, the centre having a fountain surrounded by green,—oranges, myrtles and other plants. My door (for there is no window) is propped wide open, to let in the air, the sun too is streaming in, and people are passing to and fro lending to the whole scene a striking and stage-like effect. All sorts of dialects and languages fall upon my ear, Castilian, Andalusian, Italian, French and English. Of the latter there is more here than I have met elsewhere in Spain. Seville has lately attracted hither its thousands from every part of the Peninsula and the Continent generally, for the holy week is only just over and the celebrated *feria* or fair is coming on—the 18th, being the first day—when rooms are said to fetch twenty francs per diem. As I do not care for junketings and like to see a city for the first time in its normal state, I shall most probably leave it to-morrow night, and I reserve for another letter some further description of its other remarkable features.

LETTER XXXII.

SEVILLE.

THE ALCAZAR—BEAUTIFUL AZULEJOS—THE GARDENS—
EXHIBITION OF MODERN PAINTINGS — THE CITY
WALLS — HOUSE OF PILATUS—THE MUSEO — THE
WOMEN OF SEVILLE—ALAMEDA.

Seville;
April 15, 1872.

Having again spent a delightful hour or two in the cathedral, and walked all round it, which no traveller should omit to do, as portions of the exterior are singularly interesting, having also smoked a cigar and ruminated in the Court of Oranges, like that of Cordova, contiguous to the great temple and entered by a most picturesque horse-shoe arch, I bent my steps to the Alcázar, or palace of the Moorish kings, hard by and—found myself in fairy land!

They tell me it is on a grander scale than

the Alhambra at Granada,—of this I shall be able myself to judge—once in it, you care for no comparisons, you seek to make none, for the mind is filled with present, actual beauty and has no room for calculation.

On entering the first *patio*, which is of large size, whilst the eyes are lost in wonder at the charming lace-work decorations, the ears are assailed by the drowsy hum of bees which having gathered their honey from the flowers of the neighbouring gardens, store it in the hives thus made for them by the cunning hands of men who passed to their account centuries ago.

It were vain to attempt a description of this wondrous building, now sufficiently restored to enable one to comprehend its magic beauty. The impression remains upon me of a realisation of Aladdin's palace, where all the exquisite taste and ingenuity of one of the most tasty and ingenious people in the world could devise has been employed with no sparing hand. The Hall of the Ambassadors with its delicious dome is beyond all conception, and to give you an idea of the elaboration of some of the minor details, I may mention that in the adornment of the walls there are stars not bigger than half-a-crown, which are composed of thirty-two pieces of coloured porcelain, of such delicate workmanship that they might, like the Florentine mosaics, be set as a brooch. The woodwork too is perfectly marvellous. Imagine doors and inlaid shutters that have withstood twelve hundred years of summer's heat and winter's cold, and that have been spared too the ravages of the worm and more destructive barbarian man! Some of the ceilings too are perfect studies of inlaid woodwork, and one ceases to wonder, with such models before them of the skill displayed by the Spaniards in dealing with this material.

From the palace I passed into the gardens where fresh wonders awaited me. They are unlike anything I had before beheld, and are, in fact, as unique as the building to which they are attached. All the vegetation of that sunny clime is there met together, glowing under the blue sky and warm sun with that vividness of colour to which I have before alluded, but which it is far beyond my powers to record. I speak not of oranges—they have now become a common plant, every garden growing them as we grow apples in England, and even the public squares are planted with them—but the palms, the oleanders, the roses. the cacti, all in flower and each exhaling its own odorous breath fill you with wonder, so numerous are they, and so very, very beautiful.

I left this garden of Eden, like another Adam, turning many a parting glance at its varied beauties as my steps bore me unwillingly away. As I was quitting the building my eye was attracted by a notice that an exhibition of modern paintings and works by living artists was to be seen for the small charge of half a *peseta*, and with some misgiving though with awakened curiosity I walked in.

A cursory survey of the pictures on the walls confirmed my prepossessions. The only *original* works were isolated groups and figures illustrative of Spain's great passion—

the bull fight. There were *espadas* and *picadores*, *chulos* and *bandarilleros* in all the bravery of their gala costume. Some of these were not wanting in spirit, but they had nothing of special merit to recommend them. The rest were but copies of old Spanish masters, with their peculiar characteristics exaggerated or caricatured. But it is not given to every imitator to catch the sweetness of a Murillo or the soldier-like dash of a Velasquez, and the result of the most servile copying must often prove, as it did here, a lamentable failure.

On leaving the Alcazar I took a drive round the old walls, the sight of which takes you back some centuries. They appear to have been of great strength, and no doubt at the date of their completion were effective enough for defence. The squat square towers appearing at short intervals are purely Moorish, and the city viewed from a distance with the tall spire of the Giralda and other buildings appearing above the ancient walls with here a palm and there a cypress, make a very Eastern picture.

Having refreshed myself with my drive (though with some risk to my bones, owing to the wretched state of the road), and prepared my mind for the reception of fresh objects of beauty, I again plunged into the city, taking " Fairfield " on the way.

Innumerable booths, many belonging to private families for the reception of country friends, were being run up in all directions. Skeletons of swings, roundabouts, and dancing saloons of a similar character to those with which we are so familiar at home were everywhere visible; and altogether the scene was so like Epsom downs a day or two before the Derby, or Charlton or Greenwich fairs in their palmy days, that I am inclined to believe, what I was assured on more than one hand, that the reputation of Seville fair, at least for originality, was infinitely greater than it actually merited. As far as the mere accessories are concerned, my informants were doubtless perfectly right, but the great charm to the stranger, with an eye to the picturesque, must, I take it, lie in the diversity of costume, for the *feria* is a perfect camp, and draws its contingent from every village and town for miles around, some to make purchases, others to seek gaiety, and all, more or less, to get the one " outing " of the year—looked forward to and eagerly counted upon for months before its advent.

My driver, who for stupidity and lack of knowledge of his own town beat every coachman it was ever my fate to ride behind, after driving me up three *culs de sac*, in his attempt to seek a thoroughfare, landed me at last at the house known as that of Pilatus.

Built in imitation of the Moor it possesses much to call forth admiration and study. A beautiful *patio*, and a magnificent staircase are sure to attract as they deserve admiration, and there are hundreds of *azulejos* or those celebrated tiles, which owe their origin to the Moors and were produced in high perfection in the time of Charles the Fifth.

The *Museo* will well repay almost any time that is spent upon it. There Murillo may be studied in his various stages, and with a better chance of gratification than can be derived from an attempt to examine the works of this grand painter in the cathedral or elsewhere, as the light is of course more favorable. Still, as many of these paintings were originally altarpieces and destined for certain positions, to be viewed only from particular points or at predetermined heights, they lose in one respect what they gain in another, and this will account in a great measure for what appears to be at times defective drawing. The colouring is, as usual with Murillo, superbly harmonious, but the close examination I was able to make of his fair Saints and sweet Madonnas only confirmed the opinion I expressed when speaking of this artist from Madrid; namely, that he could portray exquisite women, but lacked the inspiration to produce that divine beauty which was so remarkable among some of the great Italian painters.

I have now also had a fair opportunity of seeing the celebrated Andalusian women in the flesh, and—I am very disappointed. It is true that their peculiar characteristics are gone, and we all know how much those have to do with imparting a special charm. Their short national dresses have yielded to the levelling fashions of France. Their feet, which used to be encased in pretty shoes, have been unable to resist the attractions of the Parisian *bottine* with a so-called military heel, and as a natural consequence, instead of the famous walk—that peculiar gait which induced the belief that only an Andalusian knew how to tread the earth—the women now hobble along, and twist their hips with the exertion of preventing themselves toppling on to their noses in a manner which is anything but graceful. They are, in fact, now far worse off, and in my mind have an infinitely less *dégagée* and stately gait than the women of England, for the simple reason that the latter have a proper pavement to walk upon, whilst the poor *Sevillanas* are compelled to toddle and totter over flints with the sharpest edge stuck uppermost, which are trying under most favorable circumstances, and prove a frightful ordeal when the toes are cramped in a narrow boot with a peg in the middle three inches high.

Many of them have fine figures and most

beautiful eyes, but the rest of the features are coarse. The eyebrows are often thick and heavy as those of a man. Their teeth are for the most part small, but they have, in common with the generality of the Spanish women I have seen, that unhappy configuration of jaw which, in laughing, displays the whole of the upper gum, and when the teeth are irregular and decayed, which is frequently the case, the effect is disastrous to beauty, they get very stout at an early age, say about thirty, and the obesity of some of them is truly extraordinary.

The Alameda beside the Guadalquiver is of course the great place for the display of fashion and finery, and when the heat of the day is over, the seats and walks are crowded. Many prolong their stay to an advanced hour, and on balmy nights such as one frequently enjoys in this beautiful climate, some of the fair ones cannot persuade themselves to go home at all. These belong doubtless to the class whom Tom Moore describes as "maids who love the moon."

LETTER XXXIII.

XEREZ (SHERRY).

FELLOW-TRAVELLERS — ARRIVAL AT XEREZ — PECULIARITY OF XEREZ HOUSES — LOVE-MAKING — WINE STORES.

Xerez de la Frontera;
April 16, 1872.

THE three hours' journey from Seville to this town offers nothing very striking in the way of scenery. The country is for the most part flat, and with the exception of the aloes and prickly pears, the latter covered with fruit, there was little in the aspect of the landscape to remind me that I was so far south; I noticed a good many olive plantations, by the way, and an occasional group of stone pines relieved the monotony.

I had in the compartment with me a gentleman and two ladies, English, evidently residents of the wine city who had been up to Seville to make purchases. As my appearance is rather a foreign one, they, perhaps, failed to recognise in me a countryman, or perchance they were indifferent to my opinion even if they guessed me to be so; any way they carried on their conversation in English in the most unrestrained manner, and made remarks about persons and things which it would have been far better taste to keep to themselves.

A proof of the injudiciousness and *mauvais goût* of these indiscriminate criticisms was soon afforded by their talking of people with whom I was actually acquainted, and I fancy that neither party would have felt particularly pleased if I had communicated to those whom it concerned what I thus heard blurted aloud in a public conveyance and at the same time made known who were my informants.

It was dark when I reached Xerez, and at the very station I found that I had made a poor exchange for Seville. Of course my portmanteau had to be opened and examined; this seems to be the rule at every fresh town you enter, and after my things had been pulled over by a pair of very dirty hands, in presence of a little crowd of ragged men and boys, who surely had no right within the precincts of the station, not a coach or omnibus was to be had to convey my luggage and myself to the hotel. A couple of these aforesaid ragamuffins were therefore of necessity hired to carry the former whilst I traipsed on close behind, keeping a sharp look out to see that my goods and chattels were not bolted with in the darkness, an event which, judging from the aspect of my porters, struck me as far from improbable. No such catastrophe, however, occurred. They trudged on steadily before me for nearly a mile before we reached the town, and even then we had to traverse some long and tortuous streets ere the goal, the Hôtel de Xerez, was arrived at. Once there, however, I was comfortable enough. The *fonda* was kept by an Italian, and the use of that language to my landlord and the waiters, who were also from Italy, procured me prompt and even kindly attention.

Xerez has proved a singularly uninteresting place after Seville, although a man coming here with good introductions might pass a different verdict, for I observe that the town contains many substantial and comfortable-looking houses, the residents of merchants and others engaged in the wine trade. These houses are built in the same style as those of Seville and Cordova, having the open *patio* lined with flowers; their architecture like that of the town I have mentioned, is spoiled by the Andalusian custom of whitewashing them exteriorly from top to toe; in a sanitary point of view, the usage has doubtless much to recommend it, but it is destructive to picturesqueness.

There is one peculiarity, however, about these Xerez houses which I have *not* observed elsewhere, and as being in such contrast to Cordova, I cannot fail to notice it. In speaking of the low Moorish tenements of the latter city, I mentioned that there were scarcely any windows upon the street, and that the few which did exist were upon the upper floor, and were jealously latticed in, or otherwise closely screened. In Xerez, on the contrary, each house has, according to its size, two or three windows, whose sills are on the very pavement, and although they are well guarded by an iron grating, the sayings and doings of the occupants of the rooms thus situated are at the mercy of every passer-by, unless the inmates talk very low, and screen themselves with heavy drapery.

A curious result of this "convenient" arrangement became palpable to me, when, with my after-dinner cigar, I strolled through a few of the narrow and tortuous streets. At almost every third window, there stood a man, whose arms or as much of his face as the iron grating would admit were thrust within the chamber. What they were doing there I could not at first divine, but as in passing I perceived the flutter of female drapery on the other side, a light suddenly broke upon me, and I came to the conclusion that although I had got as far as Xerez, I had not got beyond the region where the old story was still fresh and new.

A ramble about the town by daylight has confirmed my impressions of last evening.

The houses are substantially built and have a look of thorough "respectability," as if they belonged to substantial well-to-do people who were conscious of the honour of paying rent and taxes. I observed several casinos or club-houses, that were, as far as I could judge, well frequented; nor is this wonderful in a place which must contain many merchants and wealthy citizens, with a marvellous lack of amusement to engage their leisure time, for Xerez strikes me as "mortally dull."

I noticed more than one half-ruinous and disestablished convent. As at Rouen, these huge structures seem to be employed as warehouses for goods. One, in the outskirts, presented nothing but the bare walls, on which I could still decipher portions of scripture history and episodes in the lives of favourite saints depicted in fresco.

There are of course many *entrepôts* for the storing of wine. The precious article is not kept below the earth in cellars as is customary with us and by which means of course, in a climate like ours, an even temperature is more easily attained, but is stored in huge sheds, raised a few feet from the ground, the walls and even the roofs of which are whitewashed, while the sun is carefully excluded by means of shutters or *persianes*, similar to those in use in Italy. By this means the interior is kept delightfully cool, and as Xerez is no doubt exempt from any lengthened or severe winters, the wine is not exposed to any great alternations of heat or cold.

I expected to find upon my table at dinner some of that same sherry, though of inferior quality, which is produced from grapes grown in the neighbourhood. Not a drop, however, of that or any other white wine was there. The same deep-red liquor, of which I have so frequently spoken, was the only wine visible, and whether it bore the name of Valdepeñas or of any other locality, the flavour was still the same.

LETTER XXXIV.

CADIZ

VINEYARDS—SALT-PANS—FIRST APPEARANCE OF CADIZ—
STREET SIGHTS—MULES—GLAZED BALCONIES—CUS-
TOM-HOUSE ARRANGEMENTS—CHARMING ALAMEDA.

Gran Hôtel de Paris, Cadiz;
April 17, 1872.

A RUN of an hour and forty minutes conveys the traveller from Xerez to Cadiz, and, as regards the distance covered, the journey might easily be performed in the odd minutes; but there are many stoppages by the way and at the junction of the Trocadero, where the line branches off to Port Royal, there was more activity than is usually seen on Spanish railways.

A good many vines are visible on quitting Xerez. Some of the vineyards are separated from each other by the ordinary cane, which makes an effective line of demarcation without encumbering the valuable soil; in other cases the plots are divided by the aloe, which also bristles along good part of the line.

On quitting this cultivated tract, the country becomes perfectly flat and sterile, until the traveller reaches an enormous naked plain, which looks like a morass extending to the sea, for the green line of the Atlantic is visible at its edge, and the masts of vessels indicate the position of Port Royal.

This uncomfortable-looking region, furrowed with ditches and scored into square shallow trenches, communicating one with another, constitutes the great salt-district, whence Spain draws her principal supplies of that necessary article. These trenches are the salt-pans, *las salinas*, into which the sea water runs, and where it is soon evaporated by the heat of the sun, leaving the crystals adhering to the sides and bottom of the pans. This rough salt is then swept up and shovelled into pyramidal heaps, which are numerous as tents on a military field, and look strangely monumental in the half light or under the rays of the moon.

The town of Cadiz is visible for some time before you reach it, as the line makes a bend similar to that of the South-Western of England on approaching Portsmouth, and for a few miles it has the high road in view, which appears bordered with a low arched wall in lieu of the customary posts.

I found the porters, coachmen, and hangers-on at the station at Cadiz, rougher —I may say more brutal — and more extortionate than any specimens of the genus porter and Jehu that I had ever met with. Almost as much was attempted to be wrung from me for the conveyance of my solitary portmanteau to the hotel as my first-class ticket had cost me from Xerez, and I would strongly urge upon all travellers who do not happen to use or find the omnibus of the hotel to convey them from the station, to make a clear bargain beforehand, inasmuch as there appears to be no tariff—as there is certainly no conscience—existing among the unsavoury *faquins* and cabdrivers.

Cadiz is well built, and like the other towns of Andalusia is a whitewashed city. The streets are narrow as usual, but they are for the most part straight. Many of them are not wanting in fine buildings, with a good deal of marble employed in their construction in the shape of pillars, terraces, and staircases. The cafés are paved with this material, and my hotel, which is situated in one of the best streets, the *Calle San Francisco*, has made a considerable use of it.

Many of the balconies are glazed and curtained in the manner I have so frequently described. My own chamber is so furnished, and I find it makes a delightful observatory, whence, screened one's-self, one may see all that is going on.

And many curious sights are presented to the eye of the stranger so perched. The narrowness of the streets prevents the use of wheeled carriages to any extent. It is only occasionally that an omnibus attached to one of the hotels or a hired coach rolls up the ill-paved causeway, making the foot passengers rush into doorways or dive into shops to avoid being crushed between the vehicle and the wall. All the work is performed by asses or mules, whose packs are arranged for the transport of every mortal thing— oil, wine, water, paving-stones, and brushwood. The last-mentioned article when being so conveyed is more formidable than a waggon would be, for it often, literally, reaches from one side of the road to the other, and sweeps a clean passage for itself. These same mules and donkeys—the latter being very nearly as large as the mules themselves—seem most hardy and patient brutes, without, as far as my observation goes, exhibiting the slightest symptoms of obstinacy or viciousness. They do their work like good citizens, and are often, to my mind, more lovable than their masters, whom they carry single, double, nay, even treble, when they have no other load. It is a common occurrence to see two men seated on a mule —often a man and woman—and in the country districts, as the train runs on, you will observe that the mule or ass constitutes the only means of travel to the mass of the people, which of course is not surprising in a place where tracks, only fitted for such animals, connect even large villages together.

The port of Cadiz being conveniently situated for trade is visited by vessels of all nations; hence, the most various costumes are visible in the streets, for their wearers, the foreigners, considerably swell the numbers of natives who flock in from the surrounding districts. From my elevated "box" I behold Algerines, male and female, the latter wearing a kind of high cap of gold filigree, and both sexes arrayed in gorgeous colours. I see Greek sailors with red fezzes and green baggy trowsers, their black mustachios stiffly curled over their bronzed faces, and looking as much like pirates as any painter or costumier could make them. Turks follow Americans, whose heels again are trodden on by sandalled peasants from the interior, who, though boasting never a stocking, have shawls or wraps over their shoulders that I have heard more than one dainty English lady covet.

But where are the famous Cadiz beauties whom I have been taught in fancy to admire ever since I was old enough to read my Byron? Alas and alack! that tastes should differ, or that the reality should fall so far short of the expectation! Persistently have I cast my eyes about me to discover one, but *one* solitary *one*, face or figure that I could pronounce beautiful — charming — pretty— even passable—in vain. I have been more unfortunate in Cadiz than elsewhere, arising, perhaps, from the pure perversity of things, and have utterly failed in my quest for beauty. As to their walk, I have already spoken of *that* in referring to the ladies of Seville, and I do not find their gait improved at Cadiz.

My curtained retreat reveals to me hosts of idlers who, as far as I can judge, spend almost all the hours of daylight in the streets. First, there are the vagrants proper, the irrepressible beggars who are as picturesque, as filthy, as persistent, and as numerous as I have noticed them elsewhere. They seem like spiders to have holes into which to retreat, and out of which they pop, as if by magic, when a fly or, in other terms, a stranger comes in sight. Whatever tone of voice, nature may have originally bestowed upon these wretches, they all adopt in plying their trade a certain professional whine, which one recognises a dozen yards off as proper to one of the confraternity. If a sensitive man imagines that the blessings or curses of these romantic-looking vagabonds count for anything, he may strike a pretty even balance in favour of his soul by feeing one half of the tribe, and turning a deaf ear to the solicitations of the other moiety; for my own part I confess myself to be perfectly callous so far as beggars are concerned; I never give a *cuarto* to one of them and take my curses (of course I never get any blessings) with proper equanimity.

But the mendicants, numerous as they are, form but a small proportion of the idlers referred to. There are the loungers about the hotel door, occasionally swelled by the presence of some of the waiters. All sorts of characters seem to congregate there, *valets de place*, boatmen, coachmen, couriers, and assistants from the shops on either side of the way. The amount of cigarettes they make and get through is something astonishing, but there is little *waste*. I have seen more than one half-finished cigarette stuck into the hat, or thrust into the sash that is worn about the body, to be finished at a more convenient opportunity.

The women in this part of the world seem to get through far more work, and, indeed, have very much more imposed upon them than the men. It is not that they are less fond of a gossip than their lords; but they manage to make their hands keep time to the accompaniment of their voices and thus combine business with pleasure in an equal degree. The men, on the contrary, like to make their pleasures double, and must have their smoke with which to season their endless chatter.

My Seville friends arrived last night, and we have been visiting the town together. The cathedral is a comparatively modern one and is of the Corinthian order of architecture. Ford who delights in antiquity, and who describes in such glowing language his love of the Gothic is, I think, too severe in his criticism of this temple, which is certainly not wanting in grandeur. Some of the pillars are particularly fine, and the general effect of the interior is imposing. The windows, however, are only fitted for a workshop, being plastered over with green wash, whether to imitate coloured glass or not, I cannot say; if that be the idea, the attempt at deception is about as successful as that of the man who dyes his whiskers, or wears a wig, under the impression that the cheat cannot be detected.

A busy scene was disclosed to view by our mounting on to the rampart which, as at Barcelona, overlooks the port. Many vessels were there moored, boats were passing to and fro, steamers were arriving and departing, and immediately beneath us we perceived some passengers who had just been landed from the Gibraltar boat.

The confusion and contention were positively disgraceful. There was no order and no police. The vagabond boatmen were extorting by wild looks, gestures and language as much coin out of the bewildered and tired passengers as the fears or purses of the latter would allow, whilst the luggage was being overhauled by grimy custom-house officials who performed their duty with virtuous severity or did not perform it at all according to *circumstances*; such circumstances being represented by a *peseta* or so, slipped into the expectant palm.

As the whole of our party intended leaving for Gibraltar next morning, the scene enacting below was not without its interest to us, although the active courier in Mr. P—'s service would relieve him and his friends from all personal contact with the extortionate and lawless vagabonds.

A stroll we took on the extensive Alameda will dwell long in my remembrance in connexion with Cadiz. Situated high above the sea, of which it commands extensive views, planted with trees, and richly furnished with flowers, it is a delightful promenade, and must be an immense boon to the people in the summer nights, when, after sun-down, the gentle breeze comes stealing across the water to cool the baked, and cracking soil. Only those who have spent a summer in these southern climes can appreciate to the full, the value of such a walk as this. But at Cadiz, there are few weeks in the year, when such a promenade ceases, on account of weather, to be most enjoyable.

LETTER XXXV.

GIBRALTAR.

BAY OF CADIZ—THE VOYAGE—TRAFALGAR—TARIFA—
ALGESIRAS—CONFUSION AT LANDING—TRANSFORMA-
TION SCENE.

Club-House Hotel, Gibraltar;
April 18, 1872.

You would have found it somewhat of a trial this morning, to turn out of bed at half past four, under a chilly gray sky and dropping rain, in order to be first jolted down to the port, there to embark in a small boat, for a row of three quarters of a mile to a low-hulled, not over attractive looking Spanish steamer, the "Adriano" which lay rolling in a lazy manner, whilst the men were feeding her with cargo.

Our party magnanimously determined not to go below, so every one made him or herself as comfortable on deck as circumstances would allow. The vessel was announced to start at half past six and did really get off at seven, but she proved so slow, that instead of eight hours, the advertised time, we were rather more than eleven completing the voyage. She rolled heavily and made greater part of the passengers sick. I was myself qualmish and ill at ease, but sufficiently alert to watch every interesting bit of land we passed; and as these little steamers always hug the shore, we could make out even the cattle grazing in the pastures.

The bay of Cadiz looks imposing from the sea, and the city which clusters down to the water's edge, and climbs up the adjacent heights has a fine appearance, promising indeed, more than it performs. Its white houses were on that particular occasion more than usually conspicuous owing to a dark and lowering sky which threw them into strong relief and made some of the square blocks in the direction of the Alameda look wonderfully sharp and well-defined.

Towards noon we were abreast of that cape whose name makes the most pacific

Englishman's heart beat quicker, "Trafalgar!" Even the ladies of our party, to some of whom the mere action of lifting the head, was a pain and trouble, yet rose up to gaze upon the spot, made memorable for all time; and anecdotes of Nelson, which had lain half forgotten in the mind, were raked to light and made subjects for pleasant converse.

From that point the mountainous shore is very fine and bold, and it was interesting to watch the changes produced in their shape as point after point of land was successively reached, and rounded.

We discharged a passenger or two and some luggage into a boat off Tarifa, a picturesque looking Moorish town at the entrance of the straits, with an ancient Alcázar, looking solid and stern, as those buildings invariably do, and a few palm trees rising exactly in the places where an artist would have stuck them.

A little later on, through the rather heavy atmosphere, we observed the stupendous heights of the African shore, and on the left the *great rock*, to which our eyes were constantly directed as we steered towards it.

Having put out the greater part of our fellow-travellers and goods at Algesiras, an operation which occupied a full hour, we directed our course across the bay, and dropping anchor at a convenient distance, were at once surrounded by a score of boats, from whose occupants a perfect babel of tongues suddenly issued, the English being of that peculiar kind known as " pigeon," a species of *lingua franca* that is more expressive than elegant. Mr. P—'s courier having for the conveyance of our party, made a proper bargain (a very necessary arrangement, by the bye, for the Gibraltar boatmen are not a whit more honest or moderate in their demands than their *confrères* at Cadiz), we were soon stowed with our luggage on board a couple of boats and in due course reached the landing place.

The same scene of confusion and uproar ensued there as I had noticed at the last-mentioned port, and what with the vociferations and crowding of touters and porters, it was with some difficulty that we effected a landing.

Having passed the gate and gaily responded "Of course" to the inquiry whether we were British subjects, we entered the street leading into the town, and found ourselves, as if by enchantment transported into another region, something in the aspect of its houses like the "old country," with mongrel additions of all kinds producing an effect at once strange and interesting, but in such extraordinary contrast to the land we had left only a few hours before that we felt perfectly bewildered and stared about us as in a dream.

In order to appreciate this singular effect to the full, you must have been wandering, as we have done for some weeks, among the old cities of the Peninsula, with their mediæval houses, antique ecclesiastical buildings and Moorish palaces, and amid a population retaining much that belongs to the remote past. A short sea voyage has sufficed to change the whole aspect of the scene; we behold brick houses, with the sash windows and "short curtains" of the Old Kent Road, or Islington; Smith, tailor, or Brown, bootmaker stands next to an edifice marvellously like a "little Bethel," while the familiar redcoats pace the narrow footway, and pretty girls in tightly fitting habits, their fair ringlets waving down their backs, trot past on their way to the Alameda. The confusion of ideas thus engendered cannot pass so easily away. We had obtained rooms at the Club House Hotel, the best in the place, which it may well be, and yet offer nothing remarkable in the way of luxury. Some of our party think there is one advantage about it, and that is a very *negative* one, viz. that it is more English than foreign ; but the coming here, and in the very midst of your Spanish experiences, the finding yourself in *Commercial Square,* surrounded by shops, exhibiting the well-known window tickets of the old country, seems an anomaly, and as I said before, produces such a muddle in your brain, that you require some little time to martial your ideas in order.

This at least will excuse the jerky nature

of the above remarks. When I write my next, I may perhaps have recovered somewhat from my state of confusion. At present I must confess to a feeling of grand uncertainty as to whether I am in the old world or the new.

LETTER XXXVI.

GIBRALTAR.

VISIT TO THE ROCK—FINE VIEWS—THE SIGNAL BATTERY—
THE APES—WEALTH OF VEGETATION—COCKNEY HOUSES.

Club-House Hotel, Gibraltar;
April 19, 1872.

I HAVE been over and through "the Rock" this morning and have been so delighted with the excursion, that I am about to try to make you a participator in my pleasure.

Mr. P—, having a letter for some high military authority, obtained an order for us to visit the wonderful excavations which perforate the solid rock and convert it into an impregnable fortress, the guns pointing through the holes in the outer crust on to the waters below, and threatening with destruction any object within range.

The ascent being a severe one, Mrs. P— and Miss T—were mounted on donkeys, which were furnished with a sort of armchair, on which the ladies sat, not askew, but at right angles to the animal. Mr. P—, myself, and the courier, Francesco, accompanied by an orderly, our guide, went on foot.

Passage after passage was unlocked, we constantly ascending until they were all passed through. The most remarkable of these excavations is " St. George's Hall," a huge cavern, where we were told Nelson was entertained at a banquet. The dates 1783 and 1785 frequently occur, showing the periods of the execution of the works. The Rock came into our possession, if I remember rightly, in 1704, when it was taken by Sir George Rooke.

Most extensive views are obtained from every embrasure, now of the Alantic, now of the Mediterranean, and the town of Algesiras, on the opposite side of the bay, gleamed whitely in the sunshine.

On emerging from these mysterious galleries which were carefully locked behind us, we began scaling the precipitous and rough path which leads to the summit of the rock, stopping now and then to admire and gather the brilliant wild flowers, the palmettoes, the thyme and lavender, and innumerable plants, to us unknown, with which the rock abounds (they say there are 400 varieties); and after these rests and digressions, we at length reached the central apex on which there is a battery, called "the Signal," a house, inhabited by a non-commissoned officer, whose wife, a comely and placid-looking Englishwoman, supplies the wants of adventurous visitors with " bread, biscuits, cheese, butter, and beer ;" whilst her boys, white-headed rogues of six or eight years growth, gambol with the goats or learn to be soldiers.

I cannot convey to you in words the grandeur of the view from this elevated position which occupies the centre of the three eminences by which the rock is distinguished. As you look down the frightful depth you observe the rock stand like an island, the waters of the Atlantic washing it on one side, and that ocean and the Mediterranean together on two others. It is only connected with Spain by means of a perfectly flat, sandy isthmus which they call the " neutral ground," and which can, I believe, be put under water if needful, so as to cut off all communication with the main-land. This is the exercising ground of the soldiers, the riding place of equestrians, and those who have the time prolong their canter right round the bay to Algesiras on the opposite side.

The tremendous range of mountains on the African coast looked grand from this elevation; and I should think the prospect, of its kind, must be quite as striking, and perhaps far bolder than that other famous view of the European and Asiatic shores, praised so highly by Lady Mary Wortley Montague, and referred to by Byron.

An exclamation from one of our party, "There is a monkey!" made us all rush to the parapet wall, for it has actually been denied by many that these animals still exist upon the rock. There was no doubt about it, however, in our minds, for there he was. About a hundred feet below us, a good-sized, *tailless* ape was seen busily engaged in picking something out of a hole and eating it, occasionally varying his occupation by scratching his head, perhaps in a fit of perplexity. To him shortly after appeared one, two, three, four, indeed in all, we saw six, mostly young, or at least smaller than the industrious individual first espied.

We spent an hour on this height, and then commenced our descent by another path which took us to an enormous stalactite cavern, known as St. Michael's. Unfortunately we could not get in, the lock of the gate being hampered; but Mr. P— and I, conducted by a corporal, clambered up to another entrance where we were gratified by seeing one of these wonderful productions of nature, the stalactites appearing now like the pipes of an organ, now like the twisted or clustered pillars of a cathedral, and with here and there depths so great, that a stone pitched into them was heard to reverberate as it struck from side to side for some seconds before it reached the bottom.

When we had descended sufficiently to reach the habitable portion of the rock, we came upon a richness of vegetation which filled us all with surprise and admiration. There were hedges of the richest geraniums, which any might pluck who chose. The palm, the palmetto, the fig, the orange, the lemon, the vine, all were growing almost without culture; and the roses, of every variety and colour, vied with the orange blossom and the flowering acacia in scenting the air. Conceive the beauty of a mass of prickly pear, covering yards of ground, intertwined with scarlet and pink geranium and shaded with enormous blush roses.

The enthusiastic admiration felt and expressd by most of us at sight of this prodigal wealth of nature was, however, considerably checked on beholding the houses which had been planted in its midst. The " eternal fitness of things" required that dainty or quaint abodes should spring from out this paradise of flowers and glowing colours, such habitations as French and Chinese taste would have erected there. But what did we see in lieu of these? One-storied brick houses with red tiled roofs, and with no more ornament or *feeling* about them than if they were placed upon a bare common; in fact, own brothers or *sisters*, if houses are feminine, to scores and scores of eight-roomed tenements standing in grim rows in Bermondsey or Peckham.

I never felt so ashamed of my countrymen before.

LETTER XXXVII.

MALAGA

ROUGH PASSAGE—THE CARABINEERS—MARBILLA—DIFFI-
CULTIES OF LANDING—ASPECTS OF THE TOWN—
NARROWNESS OF THE STREETS—WANT OF DRAINAGE—
DEMOCRATIC BEHAVIOUR—CATHEDRAL—FINE VIEW.

Malaga;
April 21, 1872.

If my last two letters from Gibraltar reached you in safety, you may have been struck at the familiar appearance of Her Majesty's postage-stamps on the envelopes, and perhaps thought that I had reached the old country again when in fact I was furthest removed from it. I have travelled a good many miles nearer to you since then, and when I left the old rock I was commencing my journey homewards.

We had a very stiff voyage yesterday, the seas being tremendously heavy and the old steamer (the same in which we had made the voyage from Cadiz) rolled and staggered under them, although she brought us to our destination in safety in about ten hours. It blew so hard during the night before, that we all went to bed under the persuasion that the vessel would not leave in the morning, but we were duly aroused at four o'clock, and informed that the sea had a little calmed and that the voyage would be made.

From a little town about midway, a large boat put off, having on board some fourteen carabineers with their captain and lieutenant. These we shipped for conveyance to Malaga, they being on their way back from an expedition against some bandits, or as some pretend, Carlists, who had been committing depredations in the neighbourhood, and had taken refuge in the mountains. One of the party had been left behind killed, and another of the troop was wounded, but I could not learn whether the predatory band had been broken up. I fancy from the reticence displayed, that it had simply been dispersed to reform in another district. The guards had captured one of these fellows' firelocks, and brought it off as a trophy. It was put together in the very roughest way, the stock not being even rounded or smoothed, and the wonder to me was that it could ever have been fired without blowing up its discharger.

The mountain scenery, as we proceeded, was simply magnificent. In the direction of Granada we beheld the Sierra Nevada range, the well-known mount itself being thickly capped with snow.

Some of our passengers were bound for a little place called Marbilla, but the sea was running so high that no boat could venture out to fetch them, and the travellers, much against their will, were carried on to Malaga to try their luck again on the steamer's return voyage. If this weather last they run a chance of being conveyed back to Gibraltar, and thus put in practice the game of the Irish friends, who "insisted upon seeing each other home all night."

The worst part of these sea-trips in the Mediterranean is the embarking and landing in small boats. Not only are the boatmen most exorbitant in their charges (a precious set of rascals, the whole of them), but when the sea is high there is positive danger in the process. It was with great difficulty that the ladies could be got into the boat at all from the steamer, so agitated was the water, and when they were in, there was a longish track of harbour to be traversed, into which the wind, being eastward, was directly blowing, and where we danced finely—anything but an agreeable operation after ten hours' severe tossing on board. "All's well," however, "that ends well"—we got ashore in safety, and thanks to a telegram forwarded by Mr. P—'s courier to the hotel-keeper, a carriage was waiting at the landing-place into which the ladies and ourselves were quickly stowed, thus escaping the inextricable confusion of the quay, the touters, porters, custom-house. officials, and the rabble generally, with which the doughty Francesco was left to battle. It was with quite a sigh of relief that we were whisked away from the babel of foul tongues.

The town is situated upon the sea-shore,

and is surrounded on all sides but the one which looks upon the Mediterranean by lofty mountains.

The craggy mount most contiguous to the city is crowned with an ancient Moorish castle, whose walls straggle down the height in zig-zag fashion. The gateway, visible soon after the ascent is commenced, is a fine horse-shoe arch, supposed to be *ornamented* with Roman columns obtained from some other locality, and *adorned* with coarse Roman Catholic images.

Other traces of the Moors are visible in the town. The most beautiful is another arch of white marble, giving entrance in former times to the arsenal, of which nothing now is left. One of the churches, that of *Santiago*, was originally a mosque, whereof a brick tower and some *azulejos* still remain. A river, the Guadalmedina, runs through the city. Judging from the width of its bed, it must occasionally be a fierce stream, though I crossed it without wetting my feet, and found tents erected and a cattle-market in full swing on the dry stones.

So narrow are the streets that, as usual, very few are fitted for wheeled carriages, and those that traverse them can only do so in one direction, as it would be impossible for two to pass each other. Those *calles* which are broad enough to allow of such a limited thoroughfare, have an announcement at the entrance publishing the fact, with the representation of an arrow showing the direction in which the wheeled vehicles are permitted to go. It is fortunate, indeed, that this privilege is so limited, or some of them, with the unlucky beasts between the shafts, would inevitably come to grief, not only on account of the wretched pavement, but also because of the inefficient state of the sewer traps. These are nothing but huge, circular stones, not flat to the level of the roadway, but sticking up in the centre like a shield or boss, and I observed many of them to be broken so that a foot could easily slip through; nay, some were actually tilted on one side, thus permitting all the effluvium to escape into the narrow street. Conceive the abomination of not only having such a contrivance immediately beneath one's nose all day long, which is the case with the shopkeepers in the vicinity, but sleeping, as they must inevitably do, in such an atmosphere. After this I need scarcely say that the interior of the town is excessively unsavory, and renders a stroll about its streets anything but pleasant.

Of what service is a delicious climate with pure skies and a soil teeming with luxurious vegetation, if so little pains be taken to observe the simplest rules of salubrity?

Malaga appears a small town compared with Cadiz, although there is little difference in the population of the two. It has its small Alameda, bordered with stunted trees, having a marble fountain at each end, some marble seats, statues, and busts. Here the best houses are situated, and among others, the hotel from which I am writing, a really fine house, with handsome *patio* and staircase, the gallery above being glazed in.

An amusing scene occurred there half an hour ago, which was so purely Spanish that I cannot refrain from mentioning it.

Two stalwart ragamuffins had brought up some luggage from the steamer, and were waiting to be paid. Having deposited their burthen at the door of a saloon on the first-floor, they squatted down upon the nearest trunk, and having pulled out their smoking materials, each rolled up a cigarette, lighted it, and spat to their heart's content in a circle round them upon the polished marble floor with a degree of independence that the reddest of French democrats and *sans-culottes* might have admired. Talk of *liberté, egalité*, &c., why I cannot call to mind the most "bloated Tory" of my acquaintance who would have had the face to do so much.

The Alameda looked pretty this afternoon as seen from my terrace which overhangs it. Being Sunday, a band was playing nearly opposite; groups of well-dressed persons were walking to and fro, the seats were crowded and itinerant vendors of sweets and fruit were hawking their wares as at a fair. It was a good opportunity of seeing the *Malageñas*, who are described in rhyming praise as *muy halagueñas*, or very charming, for they had done their best to set off their attractions. I begin to fear I must be growing very fastidious, or very old, or very stupid, for I refused to discover their witcheries, and dared to think, as I dare to write, that they have been much overrated.

This morning we paid a visit to the cathedral, which had nothing remarkable to distinguish it, beyond the fact of its being composed of all sorts of styles, having Corinthian pillars and one Gothic door, and looking altogether too big for the tower. The façade was intended to stand between two towers, but one only is complete, the other having been stopped in its growth through some defect in its constitution, or in the means of its progenitors. The finished one Ford not improperly likens to a telescope "drawn out," but the view from its summit is superb; the sea and landscape being equally beautiful.

A ramble about the town shows how numerous are the wine stores, and points to the great staple of trade; wine, raisins, and almonds, indeed, constitute the riches of the place, and judging from the appearance of the country beyond the city gates, as visible in the way I have first mentioned, the soil must teem with fertility. A proof of the warmth of the climate is given by the successful cultivation of the sugar-cane in the neighbourhood, and bits of this same cane are sold on the stalls as a sweetmeat.

We leave to-morrow afternoon for Granada, from which place I will write again. Do not alarm yourself unnecessarily about the accounts you may read of the unsafety of the roads. The country is no doubt just now in a disturbed state, but I have traversed and retraversed the most dangerous districts without molestation and I much question whether foreigners who do not intermeddle with their " confounded politics " would be interfered with ; any way, you who know me so well, will, I am sure, give me credit for prudence not to thrust myself unnecessarily into danger, and a heart stout enough to meet it, should it appear in an unavoidable way.

LETTER XXXVIII.

MALAGA TO GRANADA.

SLOWNESS OF TRAVELLING—THE DILIGENCE JOURNEY—
PICTURESQUE GROUP—BEAUTY OF COUNTRY OUTSIDE
MALAGA—ALORA—ARRIVAL AT LOJA—A MISHAP—
FIRST IMPRESSION OF THE ALHAMBRA.

Washington Irving Hotel;
April 23, 1872.

My first care on reaching this place was to procure my letters, one of which I felt confident would be from you; and in truth, on applying at the banker's as soon as I could conveniently do so, I found your welcome lines on the sixteenth, that is, precisely a week ago. You had then only just received my letter from Madrid, but ere this reaches you, I hope many others will have come to hand, and enable you to trace my wanderings thus far.

You seem to infer that I concealed from you the length of time I intended to be absent, but, indeed, in this you do me but scant justice. I was utterly ignorant of the time required to perform this journey. I had heard from others of the unconscionable delays attending locomotion in Spain, but I fondly hoped that as railway communication was established, many of the complaints of former travellers would prove to be out of date. I could not foresee, although I might have conceived, that with a people so inert as the Spaniards, a railway service might be introduced and yet be conducted on a system entirely different to anything else in Europe, that the rate of speed would be ten miles an hour (that of the old mail coach in England), and the stoppages at each petty station dependent, apparently, upon no other rule than that of the officials' caprice, and thus ranging from five minutes to an hour and a quarter. We were nearly thirteen hours, for instance, performing the journey from Malaga hither, having left at three in the afternoon of yesterday and arriving at Granada at four this morning, which was five up here at the hotel, and yet the distance is barely ninety miles, making just *seven miles an hour*.

It must, however, be admitted that three hours and a half were given to the diligence, by roads which I hope, for the sake of my bones, I may never have to traverse again. The stones over which we had to rattle were, many of them, as big as my head, they having been thrust unbroken into the holes and ruts of the road. There were three diligences. Ours, the largest, was the second in point of order and was drawn by ten mules which dragged us over those awful stones at a pace that would often have put the railway to shame, round impossible corners, with a torrent beneath the raised causeway, occasionally through water which was up to the beasts' middle, and all this in a pouring rain, the moon obscured by clouds but giving sufficient light to show a savage and dangerous country.

Mr. P—, myself, and the courier, Francesco, were in what the Spaniards call the *coupé* and the French the *impériale* or *banquette*, so had a famous view of the whole scene. I am not a particularly nervous person, but I assure you what nerves I have were put to a sharp test as we dashed through and over the obstacles of flood and field, for *road* it frequently was not, and as armed men occasionally emerged from the darkness as if to bar our passage, but really, as they were civil guards, to assure us that all was well.

One group we came upon, as we slackened our pace on ascending a hill, was worthy of Salvator Rosa's pencil. A fire was burning beneath the shelter of a huge rock, which assumed the grimmest aspect from the ruddy glare. Arms were piled and becloaked figures, whose swarthy features and sparkling eyes were intensified by the fire-light, were standing or lolling about the flame. Above them were rolling vast masses of threatening clouds, edged with silver, as the moon struggled to break through; and beyond, the mountains lay in inky shadow. We stopped for a few minutes parley, and learning that all was safe ahead, our postillions, if such a name can be applied to the tatterdemalions who accompanied us on the road, belaboured each mule in turn, and with many cries, objurgations, and not a little blasphemy, we were again in motion.

No contrast could have been greater than that offered to this romantic, but somewhat perilous, diligence journey, by the portion of country we traversed on the rail. While daylight lasted, my eyes were feasted with the most beautiful scenery I have yet beheld, Valencia not excepted. Some miles out of Malaga the richness of the vegetation surpasses belief, and the falling rain, by imparting freshness to the varied green, made it the more lovely.

No doubt this spring season is most favorable for the lover of nature, in the south. Everything is in flower, or giving promise of the coming harvest. The vivid red of the pomegranate blossom contrasts deliciously with the star-like, waxy flowers of the orange; the rose, in every variety of hue, vies with the abundant blossoms of the acacia; the figs are already large; the corn is high, the rye and barley are in ear; the vines are showing rich promise, and the wild flowers are in myriads. The orange trees are even larger than those of Valencia, and, if possible, more abundant. At one station, Alora, the favorite haunt of the Malagueños, and where there are many villas, the perfume was almost overpowering; whilst far as the eye could stretch, it embraced a valley of the richest abundance, producing "all the kindly fruits of the earth," and only stopped at a grand range of parti-coloured mountains.

A few weeks at a tasteful villa in this neighbourhood should offer a retreat fit for a Sybarite, and I cease to wonder at the Moor weeping when driven out of this Garden of Eden which his own exquisite taste had so marvellously adorned.

We were delayed an unconscionable time at Bobadilla, where a line branches off to Salinas, whilst the main runs on to Cordova. There was another detention at Salinas itself, but this was no longer than was needed to shift our luggage and ourselves to the diligences in order to undertake the journey referred to at the commencement of this letter, and as I incidentally mentioned three hours and a half were expended on the road, at the end of which time the spare lights of the ancient city of Loja came in view.

Most romantically situated it is, with fantastic mountains rising up all round it, and I should doubtless retain a pleasing memory of the place, as being the end of our diligence journey, were it not that the rain poured down so viciously as to make it, if not impossible, at least excessively unpleasant to protrude one's head beyond the friendly shelter of the leathern roof.

We were very nearly making a closer acquaintance with it owing to the excessive narrowness of its streets which brought the first diligence to grief, and for half an hour kept us in a considerable state of suspense and discomfort.

I have mentioned the recklessness with which the drivers turned rapid corners and wondered more than once at the success which carried them through. We had descended into the town at a rapid pace and rolled and jolted over the uneven and broken pavement in a way that threatened absolute dislocation, when suddenly I observed the mules of the diligence ahead of us turned sharply round, into what, in the darkness, appeared a fissure—a mere crack —between two houses, and drag the unwieldy vehicle after them. Scarcely, however, had the diligence got fairly into what I then naturally conjectured must be a *street*, than we heard a tremendous crash, followed by a volley of imprecations, whoopings and hallooings which were echoed back from the gloomy walls, and in the course of a minute or two brought scared and nightcapped visages to the dingy panes of many a window to learn the cause of the uproar.

Francesco leaped down from our high perch, for both our diligence and the one behind us were brought to a sudden stand, and soon came back with the intelligence that the pole of the leading vehicle had come into contact with the wall, owing to the absurd narrowness of the street, and smashed it most completely.

A misfortune of this nature, occurring where it did, was equally disastrous to all three vehicles. The *calle* or rather *callejo* where it occurred was the only outlet from the town, and as the railway station for which we were bound lay three quarters of a mile further on, and it was raining harder than ever, so that the street was converted into a mimic cataract, there was nothing for it but to quietly bide the reparation of the disaster.

This was done at last. By dint of a spare rope, a thick stake or two, and an end of chain, the pole was temporarily spliced, and after the delay referred to, we were again set in motion.

No other mishap occurred during our transit to the station, which must have been owing purely to good luck, for untaught by recent experience, we dashed on all the quicker for the detention, and went swaying along after we cleared the town, in a manner that threatened to detach the body of the vehicle from the wheels. At length a dim light or two in the waste of undistinguishable landscape hinted at the presence of the station, and shortly afterwards we found ourselves drawn up before a rude shed, which did temporary duty for that institution. A cup of hot coffee, poor as it was, was heartily welcome after the wet night-journey, but more welcome still was the warm corner of the railway carriage—the train waiting to convey us to Granada. It was only by looking at my watch, on reaching the end of the journey, that I had any notion of the time that had been occupied during this last part of it, for the sense of comparative comfort, after the fatigue I had undergone, kept me in a profound sleep until the cry of "Granada!" resounded in my ears.

But the journey was not even yet at an end. True, we had reached Granada, but our destination was the Alhambra, and a coach was waiting, in obedience to Francesco's telegram, to convey us thither. Our heavy luggage had to be left till daylight, so, armed merely with our bags and smaller impedimenta, we rolled off, greatly to the envy of some of our fellow-passengers who were left disputing for places in the two little omnibuses that were also in attendance.

Our horses were fresh, and conveyed us

rapidly along a dimly-lighted Alameda, through one or two streets lined with massive, ancient houses, and slackened their pace only as they commenced mounting a rather steep hill. We passed beneath an archway as if entering private grounds, and found ourselves on a well-conditioned road, planted with lofty elms, and having raised footways similarly bordered on either side, reminding me in the semi-darkness of that wonderful glade outside the Porta Romana at Florence, which leads up to Poggio Imperiale. This was equally steep, but proved less long, for some ten minutes after we had passed through the gateway I have referred to we pulled up before the door of the "Washington Irving," where warmth, light, supper, and comfortable rooms awaited us.

It was nearly six before I retired to mine, and as the rain had then ceased and daylight was beginning to make objects distinguishable, I threw open my window and leaned over the balcony, which was on a level with the tops of the trees.

Never shall I forget the scene. There was

just sufficient light to enable me to see the marble fountain which stands at the entrance of the grove, and note that from that point the road up which we had come descends rapidly. The trunks of the trees stood like silent sentinels guarding the *magic* causeway, for did it not lead up from *Granada* to the charmed ground of the *Alhambra?* The air was full of perfume; the sound of water, rushing, splashing, trickling, tinkling—such diversity of sound, indeed, as I have never hitherto heard yielded by water—seemed to rise from every direction; and each separate tree appeared to be inhabited by a nightingale who poured forth such a flood of song as it had never been my fate to listen to before.

I was charmed, bewildered, spell-bound by the combination of sweet sights and sounds. All sense of fatigue was forgotten. It was with difficulty I tore myself away from the terrace, and sought my pillow; and as I lay my head upon it and dropped off again into peaceful slumber I found myself murmuring—" I am at the gates of the Alhambra."

LETTER XXXIX.

THE ALHAMBRA.

VISIT TO THE PALACE OF THE ALHAMBRA—IMPRESSIONS—
FINE VIEWS—THE TOCADOR DE LA REINA—THE
—BATHS—P. V.

Washington Irving Hotel;
April 24, 1872.

I SCARCELY need tell you that my first visit this morning was paid to the Alhambra. I must confess to the being impatient as a schoolboy in view of some promised treat till I was fairly on the way thither; but, then, the idea of seeing the Alhambra with my own eyes has been to me for years a kind of daydream, and from this morning on which I have visited it, I mark an epoch in my life.

A short five minutes carried me from the hotel up an easy ascent, lined with trees, to the double horseshoe arch—the Gate of Justice—which marks the entrance to the charmed ground. I observed the "open hand" and "key" engraved upon the portal, symbols that have given rise to so much learned, but unsatisfactory conjecture, and passing through a second gate and narrow passage, calculated from their arrangement to be specially uncomfortable to an invading enemy, found myself in an open *plaza* with a palace on the one hand, and a massive fortress with square towers on the other.

As yet the Alhambra proper was invisible. The palace on the right was the vast building commenced by Charles V, and for the erection of which so much exquisite Moorish work was destroyed. Itself unfinished, it presents only the appearance of a magnificent arena for the exhibition of the national sport, and I had much ado to divest myself of the idea that the great circular *patio* was intended for bull-fighting. Anywhere else the large proportions of this building would excite surprise, and perhaps admiration, but standing where it stands, and knowing what it has displaced, I could not help likening it to a huge wen.

It is by a little simple door on the left of this colossal mistake that the stranger enters the fairy retreat of the Moorish kings, and truly, almost as the portal closes behind him, he has passed into another region.

I would fain try to convey to you some portion of the delight and deep interest I experienced in wandering through the halls and *patios* of this delicious palace, now sufficiently restored to convey some notion of what it must have been in the days when it was at once the residence and stronghold of Boabdil. But mere words, that can only produce each separate feature in detail, seem so cold and senseless when they are employed to present a picture, *as a whole*, to another intelligence.

I suppose there is scarce a monument or a scene on earth, concerning which we have read and heard much and formed our conjectures about, that does not fall short of our expectations when we behold it in the reality. My making this remark will at once suggest to you that I have been disappointed with the Alhambra, but really the only disappointment I experienced in respect of this wondrous palace, when thus permitted in the flesh to pace its halls, arose from the comparative smallness of its proportions. Part of this effect, I believe, sprang from the profuse ornamentation of every part; for there is not an inch of space in wall or ceiling unadorned, but, doubtless, with the exception of the Hall of the Ambassadors and the Court of Lions, the apartments, whether of state or for more domestic purposes, are minute and toy-like. But what a gorgeous, tasty, fanciful, fairy toy it is! What harmony of design, what wealth of colour, where time and more destructive man have spared it sufficiently to enable an opinion to be formed!

Whilst seated in the Court of Lions and taking my fill of the delicious *coups d'œil* afforded from that central *patio*, whence I could see into the Hall of the Abencerrages on the one hand, and that of the two Sisters "*las dos hermanas*" on the other, I was struck, as many must have been before me, by the resemblance offered by the beautiful ceilings to the stalactite caverns which exist in such marvellous beauty in various parts of Europe, the very dainty white marble pillars, of which there are more than a hundred supporting the fretted arches, looking like those same stalactites where, as they so frequently do, they extend from the roof to the ground. I cannot but think the cunning architects of the time took their idea from such models, so far improving upon the original as to reduce to order and uniformity what in nature is irregular and unstudied.

I have spoken of the *Sala de los Embajadores* as an exception in point of size to the general minuteness of the other parts of the building; and truly that hall is *not* disappointing in any particular. Not only are its proportions large, its shape symmetrical, its ornamentation perfect, but it offers from its various windows views that can scarcely be surpassed for exquisite beauty and extent. The tower in which this hall is placed stands at the very edge of the precipitous rock which overlooks the valley, and the Darro washes the foot of the mount some hundreds of feet below. You can watch its course for a considerable distance; here, crossed by a bridge over which mules are passing, dwindled by the depth to mere black specks, there, beaten into creamy froth by the action of a water-wheel; you can note the opposite bank where the gypsies have their domicile, and note how they burrow, like coneys, into the soil, the face of the hill being literally honeycombed by these strange people. And your eye then wanders on to the ancient city of Granada, from whose towers and steeples come borne upon a gentle breeze the sound of bells, whilst from its busy streets is wafted the hum of human voices. And you behold all this through a framework of such exquisite beauty that you are inclined to think that fairy minds alone could have conceived and fairy fingers fashioned them.

At once the most extensive and most lovely view is obtained from the "*Tocador de la Reina*," the Queen's Toilet or Boudoir, which, although retaining none of the profuse decoration visible in other parts of the building is unsurpassed in position.

You come upon it at the end of a plain brick-paved gallery terminated by a flight of three steps and an old door. This, opened, admits you to a tiny square apartment having a marble slab in one corner perforated with holes, through which the steam of smouldering perfumes made its way, and over which the sultana is said to have stood that her clothes and person might more completely receive the subtle odour. You step from out this apartment, on whose walls are the remains of painting in the Roman style, executed by Italian artists in the reign of Carlo Quinto, on to a narrow marble terrace with a parapet four feet high which runs round three of its sides, short pillars of the same stone supporting the projecting roof. And it is from this terrace you enjoy the glorious prospect to which I have alluded.

In building this fortress-palace on the very summit of the precipitous mount, the Moorish kings, no doubt, had security in view, but these same Moors, like the monks of old, had a rare eye for the picturesque, as I have observed their castles throughout Spain, to be erected like the monasteries of the middle ages, in the most romantic and commanding sites. The walls of the Alhambra follow every inequality of the ground, and where a fine prospect was to be obtained there stood a tower or a platform whence it could be enjoyed. The *Tocador* occupies an angle and stands at the very edge of the precipice, so that, as you gaze below, your eye alights upon broken rock and parasitic plants, then the tops of the trees, looking like solid masses in their profusion of leaf; then more rocks and more trees till you find yourself, like another Gulliver, trying to discover what human occupation is going on below, where those Lilliputian figures are so busy—for your height above them is so great that it requires a keen sight to aid you in your investigations. Not only do you enjoy from that favoured boudoir, in one comprehensive glance, the detailed pictures you have admired from the Hall of the

Ambassadors, but standing, as it were, on a spur of the mount you are enabled to gaze right up the *vega*, to mark the white walls and hanging garden of the Generalife, towering even higher than you are yourself perched, and to take in the magnificent range of the Sierra Nevada covered, as its name implies, with perpetual snow. It is, in truth, an enchanting spot, and dull, indeed, must be that sense which is not moved at the presence of so lovely a prospect, viewed as it is from a building crowded with romantic and interesting historical memories.

Having taken our fill of this glorious view, and only tearing ourselves from it because there were other wonders yet to visit, we descended below and passing through another dark gallery entered the Moorish baths. The *Sala de Descano* or "Hall of Repose" has been restored to the date of its completion and shines out in all the splendour of blue, red, and gold. It is almost too gorgeous, and induces the belief that the *middle* period of this palace's existence—when the gilding was somewhat dimmed and the colours were subdued, but before man's destructive finger had fallen upon the diapered walls—must have been the age of its perfect beauty. A raised gallery hints at the occasional presence of musicians, and one may conceive the luxury of reposing in so exquisite a chamber in this southern climate, after the ordeal of an oriental bath, lulled into soft slumber by the subdued notes of music and the voices of skilled songsters.

The baths, both of the sultan and sultaná, or as they are also described, *del rey* and *del principe*, are in good preservation. We stopped frequently to examine the beautiful tiles, the *azulejo dados*, which are profuse in this part of the building, and thought at first that they dated from the period of the Moor. The letters P. V. however, upon each one of them convinced us of our error, and we applied to our guide for information. We might have guessed his reply, as it was stereotyped—everything not Moorish belonged to the time of Charles V. But what is the meaning of P. V. ? He did not know.

Nor, indeed, for the moment, could we satisfy ourselves, as we did not reflect that the Spanish name of Felipe was often converted into the Latin Philippus, and that to Philip's time these *azulejos* undoubtedly belonged. Mr. P—, in our dilemma, came to the rescue. "Have you not observed," he inquired, "that it is only down here among the baths that the tiles are so inscribed?" We admitted that we had observed it nowhere else. "Well, then," he said, "the explanation is clear, P. V. can have no other meaning than *Private Vashhouse.*" The answer made us very merry, and in this mood we passed out of the vaulted chambers into the dazzling daylight where the sun shone upon the golden oranges in the garden of Lindaraja.

LETTER XL.

THE ALHAMBRA.

CHARMING SITUATION OF THE ALHAMBRA—A VISIT BY MOONLIGHT—PERIS AT THE GATE OF PARADISE—BEAUTIFUL EFFECTS OF LIGHT—FASCINATION OF THE ALHAMBRA—THE GYPSIES.

Washington Irving Hotel;
April 25, 1872.

Now that I have seen this place with my own eyes I cease to wonder at the extraordinary interest which it has ever excited, and continues to excite, among Englishmen. *Arid* Spain is, in this lovely region, arid no longer. Instead of treeless wastes you are here surrounded with a richness of vegetation and a vividness of green hitherto only associated in my mind with the shady groves and verdure of my own dear country. Built upon a lofty mount, which it crowns, the Alhambra enjoys a delicious temperature, and its approaches are glorious avenues of elms through which the sun peeps, creating flickering patches of brightness, while the boughs of the trees give shelter to numerous nightingales, who, like their sisters "by Bendemeer's stream," pour forth floods of harmony the whole day through. The most magnificent prospects are visible from this elevation, and as one gazes from the "*Torre de la Vela*," within the precincts of the fortress, either towards the city or the opposite side of the mount in the direction of the Sierra Nevada, the heart swells with a sense of fulness at the majesty and beauty of the landscape.

At a mile or two of distance there rises from the heart of the valley a flat-topped hill on which has been bestowed the name of *El ultimo suspiro del Moro*, "the last sigh of the Moor." It was there, we are told—and I am full of faith in such matters—that *Boabdil el Chico*, after the conquest of his stronghold, paused to look back on the towers of his fairy palace, on the gardens he loved so well, on the city which had called him master from his earliest recollections, and heaved a sigh for the Eden he was quitting for ever. But the whole *vega* is full of memories which find an echo in one's brain as the names of various localities fall upon the ear. Would that they were all as tender and touching as Boabdil's wordless sorrow.

Last night, the moon being at the full, we were enabled to visit the Alhambra in the light by which it is most lovely. A special permission had to be obtained, which specified the number to be admitted, but when it was known that a party from the hotel was going, several ladies, not included in the order, determined to seek an entrance.

The moon shone with that brilliancy which only they who have seen her in the south can appreciate, but her face was frequently shut out by huge masses of flying cloud that contributed in the end not a little to the grandeur of the spectacle.

I shall not readily forget the picture that disclosed itself to my eyes as we stood in a little crowd waiting the good pleasure of the old military custodian, who, with spectacles on nose, was reading the permit, made visible to him by the light of a lantern held aloft by a soldier. I have already mentioned that the entrance to the palace is in an obscure corner, which was just then perfectly in shadow, owing to a cloud that eclipsed the moon. The only light was that which emanated from the lantern just referred to, and as its rays darted hither and thither, they fell occasionally upon the group of ladies who, aware that they could only be admitted upon sufferance, held themselves somewhat timidly apart. Their dark dresses, for all were in black silk, their mantillas which shaded their faces drawn tightly round the neck and bosom, allowing only a pale cheek or flashing eye to be visible, so struck upon my imagination, that I had no difficulty in believing that they were the spirits of Moorish princesses permitted for a time to revisit earth, and who were thus like so many Peris, seeking an entrance to their whilom Paradise.

They did get in too, but I fear that the old Peter with the keys was not immaculate, and allowed any scruples of conscience he might have felt at not being able to reconcile the number of those who entered with the figure stated on the order, to be removed in the usual way.

The scene within was worth any amount of small coin expended in the shape of bribery. The lace-work decoration, the stalactite pendants, the horseshoe arches and slender pillars were still more exquisitely beautiful beneath the silver moonbeams and in the deep night shadow than in the more honest but remorseless light of day. As I sat upon one of the steps leading into the Hall of the Ambassadors, and looked out upon the Court of Myrtles, where, in the fish-pond which runs down the centre, the stars twinkled as in another heaven—as I cast my eyes upwards to the splendid ceiling of the *sala*, made dimly visible by the tapers held aloft by our guides, and then caught glimpses of the far-off mountains as seen through the windows, or rather the embrasures, of that grand old hall, a feeling as of a dream came over me, and I strove, as I have sometimes striven in my sleep, to keep from waking, lest the fairy picture should fade too quickly away.

The Court of Lions, with its hundred slender columns, half of which were in the shadow, whilst the others twinkled in the moonlight, made a charming spectacle, and the silver beams which shone on patches of the diapered walls within the Hall of the Two Sisters seemed to do so lovingly, and to bring out in the strongest relief the perfection of mural decoration there displayed.

One may faintly conceive how enchanting these halls and courts must have appeared when prepared for some grand pageant, with lamps so cunningly arranged as to bring out all the perfection of the architecture, and to display the rich oriental costume of the guests glittering with gems, with fountains plashing, music breathing its softest notes, the air impregnated with the delicate perfume of roses, orange-blossom and myrtle thickly planted round the court, the fairy picture reflected in the mirror-like water of the pond, or broken into a thousand fragments in the mimic waves of the fountains, and a moon, such as shone out of the azure heavens last night, spectatress of the festival, which she rendered the more lovely by her queenly presence.

Even then I can fancy some few stealing away from the gorgeous scene to balcony or terrace, as I did to the Tocador, to enjoy in solemn solitude the far greater spectacle presented by the city of Granada, and the extensive *vega*, stretching for many a league into mysterious distance.

The moon was obscured by a vast mass of cloud as I leaned over the parapet and sought to distinguish in the semi-darkness the various objects that had attracted my attention during the day. Suddenly there was a break in the volume of vapour, and as the brilliant rays burst through the opening, the city became visible as by enchantment, each prominent building having sprung into existence as it were by a magician's wand, whilst river, wood, and mountain grew distinct and real.

What a scene it was, and how admirably did a score of little accessories fit in to make the picture one of perfect beauty. A hundred feet below me the nightingales were swelling their throats with liquid song, the plash of falling water made a subdued and soothing accompaniment; the hum of voices floated upwards from the city, mingled here and there with the tinkle of a guitar, the baying of a dog, or the bells of a mule passing along the road, and then the clouds, urged onward by a westerly breeze, shut out the moon, and reduced the landscape to primeval darkness.

It was with a feeling of infinite regret that I tore myself away from the charmed ground. Charmed ground, indeed, for dull beyond all measure of dulness must be the mind that is untouched by some one of the features that make up the Alhambra; where history, poetry, climate, position, all combine to constitute an earthly paradise. One meets with men who have wandered hither, attracted by the name, intending to take a cursory glance and to depart, who have become rooted here for years, and who confess that the familiarity of daily life and constant communion have failed to weaken the spell which this bright spot in the Spanish peninsula has cast over them. Bitter, indeed, must have been the tears, and deep drawn the sighs which escaped the unfortunate Moors when they bid a last adieu to the groves and towers of the Alhambra.

On our return we heard, issuing from a lower room in the hotel, the sound of a guitar played by no common hand, while a chorus of discordant voices, and the occasional nigger-like stamping of the feet upon the floor, hinted at the presence of gypsies performing their strange "rites," for I cannot call their posture-making *dancing*.

We joined the score or so of spectators who were seated round the room, and as we were now at the headquarters of the strange race, I hoped to discover something different to, and more attractive than the exhibition at Seville. This, however, was not the case. The same screeching voices, each singer endeavouring to drown the noise of her neighbour, the same indecent posturing and waving of the fingers, as if they held castanets, joined to occasional clapping of the hands, the same stamping of the feet that I had previously observed were observable on this occasion, and I looked in vain for grace or even gaiety in the performance, which then, as now, struck me as the most lugubrious of entertainments.

An exception must, however, be made in favour of the powerfully built swarthy musician, who handled his guitar in a most masterly fashion. His own voice, too, was not inharmonious when performing a solo, but when urging on the dancers to increased exertions, it rose to a harsh threatening roar.

Beyond their eyes, which were black and lustrous, the girls were about as plain a set as could well have been got together. Their gowns, which are straight from the neck to the heels, are destructive of all shape, and the figures as, with hands raised above the head, they stand posturing and attitudinising, bear a wonderful resemblance in appearance and dress to the painted effigies on Egyptian or Etruscan vases.

LETTER XLI.

GRANADA.

CATHEDRAL—CAPILLA DE LOS REYES—TOMBS OF FERDINAND AND ISABELLA—THE CARTUJA—THE ZACATIN—GIL BLAS—THE GENERALIFE—BEAUTIFUL SITUATION—LA SILLA DEL MORO.

Washington Irving Hotel;
April 26, 1872.

THIS being our last day in the south, we resolved to crowd into it as many memories as the sunny hours would allow. And truly the sun did shine most gloriously, so as to make the shady groves look doubly welcome and give increased fervour to the notes of the nightingale nestled among the elms.

Having got rid of the army of pestering beggars, principally children, who lie in wait at the door and that of the opposite hotel, "*los siete suelos,*" for the appearance of a stranger, we drove down the splendid avenue and entering the ancient city of Granada, made our way to the cathedral.

The building is imposing, from its height, but it is a strange jumble of architecture and is hampered round with miserable tenements, which give, as one may readily conceive, no additional sanctity to the edifice. The interior is, as usual, blocked up by the *coro*, and there are some statues at the angles of the *trascoro* in the costume and periwigs of Louis XIV, which are very comic. There is a grandeur, however, about the high altar which redeems many absurdities, and an immense arch opening to the *coro* is particularly bold and imposing.

The traveller, satiated as he may be with ecclesiastical buildings, or as you described yourself when in Italy, as suffering from "churches on the brain," will yet turn with delight to the *Capilla de los Reyes*, the Chapel of the Kings; for in it are contained the effigies and crumbling remains of some of the great ones of the earth. Two sepulchres stand side by side. On one are extended the marble forms of Ferdinand and Isabella; on the other those of Philip of Burgundy and Crazy Jane. Most beautiful they are, and although one may object to the appropriateness of some of the ornamentation on the tombs, there can be no question about their exquisite finish and execution. How Stothard would have revelled in them!

A low door, so low that you have to dip your head considerably in passing through it, leads down into the vault, where, immediately beneath the sepulchres above, appear the leaden coffins of the actual personages, with another smaller shell containing the remains of the young Prince Miguel. That of Ferdinand is distinguished by the letter F. Ford assures us that these coffins, though rude and misshapen are " genuine, and have never been rifled by Gaul or Ghoul." He may be right, for he very often is, and rarely makes an assertion without good grounds, but our guide assured us that Ferdinand's shell had been opened by Sebastiani, in proof of which he pointed to an irregular seam, where it had been clumsily reclosed.

The plainness of this low-browed vault,

overarching the unadorned, battered leaden cases, placed there side by side, is in strong contrast with the art splendour visible in the chapel above; yet somehow, it touched me more than the magnificence of the Panteon of the Escorial, or the costliness of the Corsini's resting place at San Giovanni Laterano in Rome.

Before an altar of the chapel are other effigies of Ferdinand and Isabella, of life-size and upon their knees, which are singularly interesting as regards portraiture, costume, and execution. Two coloured basso-relievos also cannot fail to excite attention and interest. They represent, one, the presentation of the keys of the Alhambra by Boabdil on foot to Ferdinand, Isabella, and the great Cardinal Mendoza, who are all mounted; and the other, a wholesale baptism of the Moors by monks. The figures display but little dignity. The king and queen are chubby personages, very unlike the marble effigies referred to; and the features of the cardinal's thin, ascetic face are exaggerated as in a caricature. The costume is doubtless correct, and most probably the sculptured picture is an actual representation of the two events. On those grounds alone these bas-reliefs are very precious.

A magnificent *reja* of wrought iron, with partial gilding, is another ornament of this beautiful chapel, and the entrance is marked by a Gothic portal, which is itself a study.

On leaving the chapel, which, though contiguous to the cathedral, is quite independent of it, we drove up to the suppressed *Cartuja* convent, a short distance out of the town. It is a mere shell, but kept in good and cleanly order, with extensive grounds that are neglected. All the silver work and the valuable pictures it once boasted have been stolen or removed, and its only valuables are some fine specimens of inlaid woodwork, tortoiseshell, ebony, and marble. Many slabs of the latter display curious veins and markings, in which the eye can trace as in a coal fire, or as we used to do in the marbled covers of our copy-books in the old school days, strange faces and figures. These, and a cross painted to imitate wood at the extremity of the noble *sacristia*, were pointed out by the old *custode* as evidently the most noteworthy features of the place.

For my own part I found more interest in an examination of a series of pictures, representing the persecutions of the Carthusians by our Henry VIII in 1535. Here were martyrdoms with a vengeance, in comparison with which the atrocities of his daughter Mary and the illustrations to Foxe's 'Book of Martyrs,' which were at once the delight and the horror of my childhood, appeared positively mild.

There is one street in old Granada which a man with an eye to the picturesque and with only an hour to spare ought not to omit visiting. This is the *Zacatin*, the chief place of trade, where the silversmiths congregate and where the principal shopping is effected. Such houses, such balconies, such charming ruins, such romantic dirt, and such a wealth of colour, it has rarely been my fate to behold; turn your gaze in what direction you will, and there is a picture ready to your hand.

As we drove into the *Plaza de Vibarambla*, we made our coachman pull up to take our fill of its features. It is now a market-place, once dedicated to public feasts wherein the *Jereed* and bull-fights have been displayed in the past for the various generations of Moors and Christians. The great object of interest, however, to us was the Archbishop's palace, for was it not within those walls that our old friend, Gil Blas, found such comfortable quarters, till one act of sincerity amid his life of deceit procured his ignominious expulsion? It is the finest satire throughout Le Sage's clever book, and we gazed at the portals of the old palace as though we expected to see Gil Blas' venerable master issue forth on his way to the cathedral to preach one of those very sermons the simple secretary thought fit, in an evil hour, to criticise.

At the Italian Consul's, whither we went to procure orders for the Generalife, now the property of Prince Pallavicini of Genoa, we were shown the veritable sword of Boabdil, studded with jewels, and some good pictures, in the *sala* mixed with not a little curious rubbish. On the walls I recognised some photographs—counterparts of those in my own portfolio—of that charming garden attached to the Villa Pallavicini near Genoa, the beauty and situation of which are scarcely inferior to the Alhambra itself, nay, to many, the glorious expanse of the Mediterranean on one side and the undulating ground, so richly interspersed with wood and rock on the other, offer attractions that not even this favoured region of Granada can pretend to.

There is an indescribable charm, however, hanging round the Generalife which gives it a special character. Its commanding height —for it looks down upon the Alhambra Hill and commands the whole city of Granada, with miles upon miles of the *vega*, stretching on, on, till stayed by a barrier of distant mountains—has much to do with it; its terraced gardens, tier above tier, filled with flowers that look resplendently bright and become intensely odoriferous under the beams of the southern sun, also lend their aid; the abundance of water, for the Darro, there put in requisition for the supply of fountains, and rushing swiftly through the courts beneath ever-verdant bowers, making music as it flows, contributes not a little to the delight; but apart from all these, the memories with which the place is crowded, and the many romantic tales which, true or not, have been told so often that we end by giving them credence, make the Generalife one of the most remarkable spots in the Peninsula.

One cannot help observing that a story or legend recounted in an alien atmosphere will often meet with incredulity, when it would not be, for a moment, questioned in the locality where the scene is laid. As one leans over the brink of an abyss and feels, on gazing into the depths, that creeping at the soles of the feet and whirling of the brain, which will at times affect the strongest nerves, no tale of mysterious horror is too extravagant for belief. When standing in the hall of the Abencerrages, and surrounded by objects which transport you, as it were, to a different world, few can withstand the testimony of the stained basin of the fountain, to the massacre of the devoted troop, or refuse to believe that the wailing sounds heard at midnight owe their origin to the murmurs of their unexorcised spirits rather than to the sighing of the wind through the arcades or the gurgling of water through hidden pipes and channels.

Within the charmed precincts of the Generalife no story connected with the place seems too wild for credence, no legend too romantic for one's faith. One looks with a strange curiosity on the venerable cypresses—the " trysting place " of the sultana, whose midnight meetings with the Abencerrage led to such a fearful scene of carnage, and one turns a deaf ear to the cynics who, writing from " beyond the pale," would teach us that it is all a fable.

An hour of solitary musing spent at that open colonnade, which commands the prospect I have above alluded to, would make a convert of the most sceptical.

Commanding as this position is, it is not the loftiest from which to enjoy the view.

Higher yet stands the hill-top crowned with ruins known as *la silla del Moro*—the Moor's chair—which, however, was not sufficiently lofty, or placed in a position sufficiently beautiful, to save it from the destructive hand of man. The Spanish Christian battered down the little Moorish temple to raise upon its foundation the chapel of St. Elena; and the French in turn, in parting wantonness, scrambled hither to make a greater ruin.

LETTER XLII.

FROM GRANADA TO TOLEDO.

POLITICAL RUMOURS—ANOTHER DILIGENCE JOURNEY—
SOLITUDE OF SPANISH LANDSCAPE—JAEN—MENJI-
BAR — ALCAZAR — CASTILLEJO — FIRST APPEARANCE
OF TOLEDO—ANCIENT HOUSES—DECAY AND PIC-
TURESQUENESS.

Toledo;
April 28, 1872.

RUMOURS of predatory bands scouring the country, and called brigands by some of our informants, Carlists by others, and both combined, by not a few, have formed part of our table-talk during the last day or two, so that on turning out of bed at four o'clock yesterday morning, in order to join the diligence, which was to start from the *plaza* at Granada punctually at five, we had in prospect during our eleven or twelve hours journey across country to Menjibar, on the Cordova and Madrid line, just that spice of danger which removed the trip out of the ordinary category of every day travelling.

You will judge by the date of this letter that I have performed the journey in safety, and I can now assure you that I have escaped even a meeting with these modern " free lances." There is no doubt, however, but that travelling, just now, in Spain is not without its dangers, and although a good many wayfarers may, like myself, traverse the Peninsula from end to end without molestation, they are only like the proverbial pitcher, which goes often to the well in safety, but may get " a crack " at last. All the trains are running with extra police to guard them, the cocked hat turns up in the most unexpected places; every petty station has two, three, or four civil or rural guards, who make the station-house their headquarters; it is not safe to undertake mule journeys, and, above all, those by private carriage should be eschewed. Even the diligences travel in company; all Spaniards one meets in them are armed, and heavily armed police are posted in relays all along the roads.

These facts speak volumes as to the state of the country, and require no comment. I cannot say, therefore, that I view with other than satisfaction my speedy return, for although I take as little heed of these things as most men, I should very much regret being knocked on the head in this country, where I should get miserable surgical attendance, if I were not killed outright, and but little decent respect for my body if I were.

The road to Menjibar, though exhibiting some fine mountain scenery is a particularly lonely one, running sometimes through deep ravines, and at others across open tracts of country, where there is neither land fit for cultivation nor the appearance of a human dwelling.

One can scarcely realise, till actual experience has taught the lesson, how strangely silent and solitary are these Spanish landscapes. Not only are there no inhabitants, but as for hundreds of miles the country is bare of trees and shrubs, there are neither birds nor insects, and the dead silence becomes after a time inexpressibly painful. In parts of Corsica in the island of Sardinia, and in many districts of the Italian Peninsula, one may travel the day through and not meet a human being, but at least the feathered and insect world are a-wing, and their motions and tiny voices are pleasant and soothing to the mind. In the greater part of Spain, on the other hand, the stillness is "like unto death" itself, and while the ear aches with the intensity with which it listens for some welcome sound, the eye is pained with the constant aspect of sterile rocks or bare uplands, seamed with the rains, though never a drop of moisture is left upon them, and void of every growth but a dry stick or thistle rustling in the wind.

On this particular journey, for an hour or two after we left Granada, we met a few stragglers wending their way to the market. They were doubtless peaceable subjects, though to all appearance they might have been veritable " gentlemen of the road," and travelled with strings of mules, caravan fashion, and I noticed, in more than one instance, the gun was placed in readiness across the pack-saddle. As we went on even these scanty travellers fell off, and but for the occasional appearance of the civil guards to whom I have before alluded, who emerged at times in a somewhat startling manner from behind a heap of stones or from a hollow in the road, we saw not a living soul; and yet this was the high road leading from Granada to the capital of the country.

About 1 o'clock we reached Jaen, the capital of a little kingdom of its own in the old days, and still retaining portions of the walls and towers which defended it, and having an hour at our disposal, were glad to stretch our legs and unbend our bodies from the cramped position to which they had been subjected for so long a time. This old city, considering the bareness of the surrounding country, must be a dismal residence in the *best* of seasons, and a supremely uncomfortable one in the *worst*, for the contiguous heights almost shut out the sun during the season when it is most needed.

Our party were, of course, objects of curiosity to the populace, and I could readily forgive their importunity when I reflected upon the small amount of amusement that their every-day life must naturally afford them. The arrival of strangers in the idle, sleepy old city must be, indeed, a godsend, and it was no wonder, therefore, if the *plaza* where we descended should present quite a " deadly-lively " aspect, owing to the gathering of all the oddities and idlers of the vicinity about our lumbering vehicles.

Some three hours more of jolting through a country not a whit improved in appearance brought us in sight of the railway embankment and the station at Menjibar, composed of a house and a few sheds, and after driving for a few hundred yards up an incline, over a road *projected,* but never really *made,* the diligence staggering and sinking occasionally almost to the axletrees, and threatening at every instant to topple over, we reached the firmer ground, *quittes pour la peur,* and with infinite satisfaction, descended from our high perch in the *coupé* at about five in the afternoon.

Glad as we were to reach Menjibar, we were heartily tired before we left it, owing to the train being an hour and a half late. A tolerable meal whiled away a portion of the time, and those who smoked found consolation in the consumption of "the weed," but it was weary waiting on that bleak and exposed platform, over which a chilly breeze swept unceasingly, with nothing to please the eye in the shape of green tree or shrub, and no prospect around but the dun, sun-burnt, and wind-dried landscape. With such a prospect eternally before their eyes, how can the people be otherwise than savage, morose, and melancholy?

The train hove in sight at last. But as Menjibar presents the only *buffé* (as the Spanish time-bills have it) upon the road, until long after midnight, its passengers got out to dine, and, of course, did not hurry over the operation, so that nearly three quarters of an hour more were expended before the train was again in motion, leisurely rolling us along in the direction of the capital.

Considering how the railway traffic is managed in this country, it puzzles me more and more to discover why such a system of locomotion was ever introduced into Spain, where no one is ever in a hurry and where no one seems to understand the value of time. Surely the diligence was fast enough for Iberian travellers (it is, indeed, often quite as speedy as their railway trains), or if that mode of conveyance did not suit their tastes, they might have stuck to their ambling mules and donkeys, or dislocated their bones in a springless ox-waggon, and would, I should fancy, have been just as satisfied with their progress.

It fell dark very shortly after we were in full motion, and then the comparative ease of the railway carriage, after the fatigue we had undergone, lulled us into slumber, in spite of the ugly rumours, now increased in their sensational details, of trains stopped and upset and passengers robbed and otherwise maltreated.

Without any misadventure we ran on and reached Alcazar, a great junction station, between 1 and 2 a.m. Here, in a pouring rain, I parted with my friends, they going on to Valencia and I speeding due north.

Bradshaw gives a valuable hint to travellers proceeding to Toledo from the south, not to break their journey at Castillejo (the proper junction), "where there is neither waiting-room nor buffet, but return as far as Aranjuez at which all the trains stop, where they will find refreshments." Of the pleasant aspect of Aranjuez with its running water and shady groves—a very oasis in the desert—I have already spoken, when its deliciously green woods broke upon my eye as I travelled from Valencia to Madrid. The train was, as usual, a long time coming, but it appeared at last, and landed me at about 10.30 a.m. at the ancient city from which I now write.

The first appearance of Toledo is very imposing. Built upon rocky hills, the houses rise one above another in solid blocks, with the huge square Alcazar, the fortress-palace of the Moors, crowning the vast congeries of buildings. It reminded me of one of the old mount-built cities which break so grandly on the sight between Rome and Naples, although the Spanish landscape can never boast the delicious varieties of colour which distinguish the Italian campagna.

The entrance into Toledo, over the *Alcantara*, which crosses the foaming and rushing Tagus, is no less impressive than its distant aspect. As you pass under the venerable gate-towers which guard the bridge at each end, you feel as though bidding adieu to the present age to seek the homes and people of the past, nor does this idea cease to cling to you as you wander through the tortuous streets, and observe the Moorish houses, the open-air *patios*, the balconies, ironed or latticed, filled with flowers, through which dark eyes peer at you, and the queer, knobbly, broken pavement, wholly unfit for any traffic but that of the donkey or the mule.

Some most extensive views break upon you as you climb up the terraced road, and the prospect from some of the overhanging balconies, which have the Tagus boiling hundreds of feet below them must be perfectly enchanting when the moon, which is apt to lend so flattering a light, converts heaps of black ruins and a sterile rocky soil into "things of beauty."

Moonlight is, in fact, the time to *enjoy* Toledo. Under the garish sun, the incongruous additions made by successive Christian architects to the charming creations of the Moor, are painful to the man of taste, and make him either laugh or feel indignant. The broad light of day brings out too clearly the poverty, the sloth, the dirt, the utter discomfort that lurk in every corner of this once imperial city, which, from a population of nearly a quarter of a million, cannot now boast of more than a tenth of that number. But when the moon has risen sufficiently to enable you to direct your steps in safety through the narrow crooked streets, when her beams shine upon only part of the quaint old buildings and leave the rest in mysterious shadow, when Christian symbols and Moorish ornaments become in the half-light blended into harmony, then, indeed, you admit the power and the charm of such a city, and feel all the romance within your nature, which you too hastily thought had been utterly destroyed, come welling up from its hidden depths in unsuspected vigour.

LETTER XLIII.

MADRID.

POLITICAL TROUBLES—UNEASY FEELING IN THE CAPITAL —PETTY CONDUCT OF THE GRANDEES—THE MALE POPULATION—IN THE COUNTRY AND AT MADRID.

Madrid;
April 29, 1872.

ON arriving at the capital this morning I found the station crowded with troops waiting for trains to convey them to the very district I had just left, in order to quell actual or apprehended risings of the Carlists. The passengers by our own train were eagerly questioned for news, as reports, whether true or not, had reached Madrid of most of the towns of Andalusia being under arms. Unhappy country! which, amidst its poverty and other numerous impediments to progress, has constantly to witness the strifes of political parties, whose leaders, dead to all patriotism and honorable feeling, are content to make the misery of thousands so that they may themselves play out their petty wretched game.

Besides the feeling of anxiety which these rumours of disturbance occasion in the city, I discover that the capital is far from being at ease upon its own account. Yesterday, being Sunday, a bull-fight was held here, and so confidently was it expected that a rising would take place in favour of the Carlist cause during the entertainment that several suspicious characters were arrested; and the *corrida*, instead of being attended by the usual civil guard, was watched over by a regiment of the line, fully prepared for any eventualities.

The *paseo* was, however, thronged with the usual crowd of carriages and foot passengers, and it was remarked that the King and Queen, riding as usual in their low victoria unattended, prolonged their drive till the bull-fight was over, and then quietly took their way to the palace. Surely, if pluck, manliness, and perfect confidence in the people are capable of touching their hearts, King Amadeo should secure their respect, if, as a foreigner, it be difficult to win their love.

Of *that*, indeed, there would seem to be but little chance whilst "pettinesses," such as become the common talk, distinguish many of the *grandees*. I have already alluded to the fact of their louts of valets sitting with folded arms whilst passing the King and Queen, staring at them unmoved, or appearing oblivious of their presence—behaviour which could only spring from their masters' orders to that effect. But there is one family, boasting the purest of *sangre azul* in their veins and no end of quarterings on their shield, who are guilty of a far greater breach of manners, and who show by their puerile behaviour how little they have taken to heart the great lesson that *noblesse oblige*. These distinguished personages are accustomed to delay their visit to the *paseo* till the royal pair have joined the throng, when they immediately turn out in an equipage of a more pretentious character. If the King appear in a carriage with a pair of horses, *they* drive down with *four*. If His Majesty should sport a jockey in a scarlet jacket, they will display one or even two most gorgeously attired; on one occasion, when I was present, the postillions appearing in pink silk jackets and gold-tasselled caps, the very perfection of a quack doctor's equipage at a fair. The *Madrileños* seem to think this sort of rivalry displays a fine independent spirit; for my own part, it seemed fitted only to awaken contempt and disgust.

To-day again the "Recolletos" has been crowded, and to judge from the gay equipages and merry, chatting groups lining the footways, discoursing of anything rather than politics, one can with difficulty conceive that disaffection is stalking through the land, and that these very walks and groves, intended as the resorts of pleasure and recreation may, a few hours hence, be stained with blood. And yet many things are more unlikely. This city of Madrid contains spirits as mercurial as those of Paris, and it is in the recollection of thousands whose memory is of the very shortest range that the sound of musketry has awakened them from their slumbers to the painful fact that a revolution had broken out in the capital.

Nothing, however, on this beautiful April afternoon intimated to the stranger that such a calamity was near. The dusty walks were trodden by myriad feet. The fan, like the semaphore of old, was performing all the wondrous antics of which it is capable, and delivering, like the instrument to which I have compared it, a very volume of messages to the initiated. The carriages bearing their usual freight of bare-headed or mantilla-covered ladies rolled up and down within the boundaries defined by fashion. The narrow slip placarded *aux cavaliers* was filled with riders, many of whom it is true were not at ease, although it was clear that their discomfort arose more from physical than political causes; and, in fact, all appeared to be " merry as a marriage bell."

Having now visited the greater part of Spain, I may mention in this place my general impression of its male inhabitants. The peasantry I have seen throughout the country, and the labouring classes, generally have struck me as robust and able-bodied. The military, who are drawn in a great measure from the former, are many of them of large frame, and my friend Colonel P— spoke in the highest terms of their powers of endurance, of their cheerfulness under privation, and of their amenity to discipline. As "raw material" he considered them unsurpassed upon the Continent. I cannot say so much of the inhabitants of the towns, and those of Madrid impress me as particularly undersized. Their manners, too, are in many instances rude to boorishness, and as they seem to have the very smallest consideration for the feelings of others, they are naturally wanting in the first essential of the true gentleman. For instance, a group of well-dressed men will stand in the middle of the pathway smoking, spitting and talking, and stare a lady out of countenance, whom they compel to turn aside into the dirty road and on to the painful flints which form the pavement. They will enter a railway carriage or an omnibus full of ladies with a lighted cigar in their mouths, or light one when there under similar circumstances, without a question as to whether their own self-indulgence is offensive. In fact, they seem to retain so much of the oriental character as to look upon women as inferior beings, created simply for their own pleasure and service, and one sees none of that chivalrous bearing (not even so much as the raising of the hat) towards the gentler sex which makes Don Quixote so dear to every lover of true manliness. It is not improbable, as Spaniards have so little changed since Cervantes' time, that that able writer meant, in giving this gentlemanly feeling to his hero, to read his countrymen a lesson on their deficiency in this particular. If so, the shaft has missed its aim. But there is no shield so impregnable, no armour so unassailable, as ignorance and self-conceit. A Frenchman will do a rude thing though he begs your pardon while he does it; the Spaniard is often quite as rude, but then he does not even apologise for his want of manners.

I shall be able very shortly to learn for myself the truth of the report concerning the Carlist movements and the dangers which beset even the peaceable ordinary traveller by rail, as I shall quit Madrid to-morrow by the mail train for Bordeaux, which leaves at half-past six in the evening. One part of my journey I find I must abandon, namely, a visit to Bilbao, for I observe posted up at the railway station a notice to the effect that the line is "interrupted" between Miranda and that city. (It is, *in fact*, in the hands of the insurgents). The direct road to France is reported open, and I learn that large bodies of troops have been sent along the line to keep it so. If the soldiery can only be depended upon, this storm, threatening as it now looms from every quarter, ought to blow over; but, they have an ugly knack of turning round upon th officers in times of trouble, and up?ettir by such a proceeding the nicest calculation

LETTER XLIV.

MADRID TO PARIS.

QUIET JOURNEY NORTHWARD—AN OLD ACQUAINTANCE—
HIS VIEWS OF THE STATE OF SPAIN—ADVANCING
SPRING—CLOSING REMARKS.

Paris;
May 3, 1872.

THE postmark of this letter will have shown you even before these lines are extracted from their envelope that I am once again in the gay, *toujours gaie*, capital of France, and have got out of Spain in safety.

Barring the abundant presence of the military, who were posted at every station along the road, and turned up at unexpected places all through `the` journey, there was nothing of a disturbing nature to mar our progress from Madrid northward. Still, having in our memory a recent event or two which had leaked out through the Madrid *Correspondencia*, of trains being fired upon, of rails torn up, and of stations which, when entered, were found to be in possession of a hostile band, we obtained but little sleep through the night, and observed the first appearances of dawn with undoubted satisfaction.

Whilst waiting for a few minutes at San Sebastian whom should I behold upon the platform but my good friend Colonel P—, who had just alighted from a train coming from France that was on its way to the Spanish capital.

Hasty greetings were exchanged, and I learned that having a week or two back left Saragossa for Biarritz he was now attempting to return, but found all communication stopped with the exception of the direct northern line.

"I shall go on to Madrid," he said," and try to work my way round."

" Ah, well," I observed, "from all I hear the struggle is nearly over. The Carlists are making no way, and do not appear in any instance to withstand the attacks of the troops."

" Do not believe it, my dear friend," was his answer. " Depend upon it you see only the commencement of a struggle the end of which no one can foretell. I fear the worst."

And he shook his head gloomily as we pressed each other's hands and parted.

My two months' absence had wrought a great change in the aspect of the country. That which was then bare and sterile I found on my return rejoicing in a bright garment of green, and giving promise of fertility. Nature was again awakening after her long sleep, and a few hours had sufficed to convey me from a hopeless, treeless wilderness of stones, to green pastures, running waters, and richly wooded mounds.

In casting a look back at my journey now brought to a close, so far as Spain is concerned, I would recommend every traveller who intends visiting it for the first time to enter it, as I did, at its northern extremity in order that he may have a correct notion of the extraordinary contrast presented between its northern and southern provinces. If, taking steamer to Gibraltar, he content himself with a run into Andalusia, his estimate of the Peninsula will be, perhaps, a flattering but a very false one. If, on the other hand, he take a trip from France into Madrid, and go no further south, his bitter experience will induce him to pass a judgment the direct reverse of the former. It is only by travelling through the country from end to end, and visiting the interesting Mediterranean sea-board into the bargain, that he will be able to form anything like a correct opinion of Spain as a whole; and, judging from the deep impression left upon my mind, and the fresh store of pictures stamped upon my memory through this Spanish journey, I would strongly recommend those who have the requisite means, health and time at their disposal, to try a spring trip through Spain.

THE END.

EFFINGHAM WILSON, PRINTER, ROYAL EXCHANGE.

www.ingramcontent.com/pod-product-compliance
Lightning Source LLC
Chambersburg PA
CBHW030305240426
43673CB00040B/1065